MEISNER FOR TEENS
a life of true acting

Larry Silverberg

A Smith and Kraus Book
Hanover, New Hampshire

A Smith and Kraus Book
Published by Smith and Kraus, Inc.
177 Lyme Road, Hanover, NH 03755
www.SmithandKraus.com

© 2010 by Larry Silverberg

All rights reserved. No part of this book may be reproduced in any form or by any means without the prior written consent of the author, excepting brief quotes used in reviews.

First Edition: May 2010
Manufactured in the United States of America
9 8 7 6 5 4 3 2 1

Text and cover design by Kate Mueller
Book Production by Electric Dragon Productions, Montpelier, Vermont

Library of Congress Control Number: 2010924114
ISBN: 978-1-57525-616-0 ISBN-10: 1-57525-616-9

for my family

and for every family that arises
out of a need to tell the story eight times a week and
the family who comes to witness them do it

and for sarah and ali
who light up the cover of this book
isn't it obvious, they are best friends for life

Contents

	Introduction	vii
chapter 1	This Thing Called True Acting	1
chapter 2	Approaching the Play	8
chapter 3	Want Your House to Last? Build a Strong Foundation	21
chapter 4	If You're Going to Do It, Why Not Really Do It?	29
chapter 5	The Way You See the World	37
chapter 6	What They Do Matters	45
chapter 7	Is Anything Behind Those Words?	55
chapter 8	Do You Know What You Are Talking About?	64
chapter 9	The Future of Actor Training	73
chapter 10	More Quotes to Challenge and Inspire	81
	My Acting Journal	87

Introduction

I have done a tremendous amount of traveling, teaching master classes in many parts of Europe, South America, Canada, and all across the United States. It has been an exciting journey, having the great pleasure to share the Sanford Meisner Approach with professional actors, feature film directors, screenwriters, professors, and heads of university theater departments, as well as thousands of college and high school acting students. Sometimes, we did the work in English, but often the work in class was done in the native language of the participants with the help of wonderful translators.

Not long ago, I was brought down to Sao Paulo by the internationally renowned university Fundação Armando Alvares Penteado (FAAP) to introduce the Meisner work to Brazil. In the evening of my first day there, I was to give a public symposium/master class. It was held in the school's very large auditorium where, a week before, a speech had been given by the prime minister of England on the world economy. As I walked to FAAP with a student who was sent over to my hotel to take me to the school, I wondered if many people would come, the Meisner work being basically unknown in this part of the world. As I came into the lecture hall, the place was jam-packed! Hundreds of people had come to learn more about this acting technique and, I imagined, how it compared to the methods of acting that were being taught in the country's own theater schools. But I was soon reminded of the very thing I have experienced in every part of the world where I have taught. These people had come for something much more personal and essential to them.

I did the symposium as part lecture, part demonstration with audience members doing sample exercises followed by a question-and-answer period. My main theme for the evening was "human values." I went into great depth, exploring how the Meisner work is rooted in human ways of working and how it continually calls on us to be more authentically and simply human. I also spent a lot of time uncovering the basis of our life—desire—and how this fundamental human component is also the fundamental component of the Meisner Approach, powerfully revealing itself in every step of the lengthy and meticulous series of exercises.

As we got deeper and deeper into this "conversation," I could feel a shift in the room. There was a great stillness in the audience, the kind of stillness you feel when you are sharing a moment with a loved one who is in pain and who takes your hand searching for comfort. Or the beautiful silence when you look into the eyes of your child and feel the depth of love that has made your life worth it. Well, on this evening in Sao Paulo, the audience and I had reached this kind of close contact. I realized then, and with the many comments from the audience, that the hunger for these human values we were exploring was profound and was not being addressed in the work they had been doing previously. This experience didn't surprise me. I have felt this exact hunger in every group I have worked with, and I will talk about it more specifically in my chapter on the future of actor training.

Now, I want to shift the focus to you.

First, welcome to my newest book on the Meisner Approach. I appreciate you and your interest in this work. Since my other book for teens was released, *The 7 Simple Truths of Acting*, in addition to my classes for professional actors, I have been touring the country leading my workshop called The Teen Actor Master Class. In these travels, I have worked with thousands of teen actors, and I have learned a great deal about the challenges and pressures you are experiencing and the great demands placed on your teachers who are trying to teach acting in a high school setting.

I want you to know that the very beginning steps of the Meisner Approach have great value for you. If you actually do the exercises with consistency and great commitment, your whole life will transform.

I do not say these words lightly. The thing I know about being a teen—from teaching teens, from my two teenage children, and from having been a teen myself—is that for most teens, their whole life is about their attention on themselves. Just as I was plagued with self-critical thoughts when I was a teen and worried about what other people thought about me, I know that this is also the experience of just about every teen I have ever worked with. Of course, when the attention is on oneself, true acting is impossible. This is a basic truth that most actors never face. You see, when your attention is directed at yourself, your acting instrument simply cannot function. And this is the point of my book: to help you free yourself of all restrictions to act!

To truly act, you must be free—a free human being. Just like when you were born.

By the way, if after reading this book, you find the work compelling and want to know more, I have many resources for you. First, I have a whole bunch of other books about the Meisner Approach published by Smith and Kraus. I also have many acting programs, some in the summertime, and I have visiting workshops where I come to your school. You can learn all about my books and my training programs on my websites. My main site is www.actorscraft.com; my newest site is www.meisnerteacher.com. Another site for one of my classes is www.thewaybackout.com, and then I have a website that I designed to help you find a great college acting program: www.collegeactingprograms.com.

If you have any questions about the Meisner Approach or any of my classes or training programs, please e-mail me at trueacting@actorscraft.com.

Ready to enter the book? Here's one more item. This is a workbook. The way to get real value from this book is to do all the journal work and other exercises I assign to you. OK? Then let's continue . . .

chapter 1

This Thing Called True Acting

The purpose of this book is to explore with you the art of true acting. The path toward this wonderful craft will be the Sanford Meisner Approach.

Please get a notebook (or you can use the space provided in this workbook) and use it for the writing exercises I will be giving you from time to time throughout our talks together. You can call this your private acting journal because I don't want you to share what you write down with anyone—unless you choose to, of course. This is private and just for yourself. If you actually do the assignments, it will make your time with me more valuable.

I will give a broader conversation about true acting in chapter 8, but right now, I have a writing exercise for you.

 Your first assignment is to write the words **true** and **false** at the top of a page. Then, under each of those words, write as many words as you can think of that relate to true or false. Do that now, and then go to the next page to see my lists.

True	**False**
_____	_____
_____	_____
_____	_____
_____	_____
_____	_____

True	False
genuine	fraudulent
authentic	counterfeit
honest	fabricated
direct	two-faced
frank	faithless
candid	sham
real	fraud
earnest	imitation
open	rip-off
natural	dupe
unaffected	bogus
actual	invalid
legit	inauthentic
heartfelt	phony
unfeigned	artificial
devoted	affected
trustworthy	fake
reliable	pretended
unwavering	unconvincing
faithful	misguided
realistic	fabricated
legitimate	fictitious
rightful	unfounded
unelaborated	untrue
unvarnished	deceitful
sincere	unreliable

Please review your two lists of words, then look again at mine and answer this question: If you are going to act, which list do you want your acting to be most related to?

I don't know about you, but when I am in the presence of theater that is false, my mind will wander off to more interesting things: something that my daughter told me she is dealing with at college, the banana waffles I will cook for breakfast tomorrow, the wild hair on that lady sitting next to me.

> There is no god higher than truth.
> —Mahatma Gandhi

WHY DO YOU WANT TO DO THIS?

You know, it's much easier (and cheaper) to stick a DVD in the DVD player or log onto YouTube than go see a play. Why, then, do you suppose people still bother to see live theater? There is only one reason: People go to the theater hoping to have an experience that will change their lives. What does that mean, "to change their lives"? It means that in the intense pressure of daily living that most people experience, the need to produce results right now and with a technological world that does not encourage intimate relationships, people ache to be reminded that they are, in fact, human beings.

The question for actors, then, is how do we offer this kind of experience to the people who come to see us work? My answer: It has everything to do with bringing life to the stage.

You may be wondering, at this point, just who I am and how I arrived at the ideas I am going to be sharing with you. I was very fortunate. I studied with the greatest acting teacher of our time, Sanford Meisner. Most everything I have done in my adult life has sprung from the fire that Sandy lit inside me during the years I spent with him and my classmates at the Neighborhood Playhouse in New York City. So, if the idea of becoming a true actor and bringing life to the stage sounds tasty to you, let's continue.

What's Driving You?

Here is another important word for actors: **hunger**. What do you think that has to do with acting? Take a few minutes to think about it, and then in your journal, write down what you think hunger has to do with acting. Do that now, I'll wait.

_____

_____

For me, when I hear the word *hunger* in relation to acting. I think of a powerful desire, a craving that demands to be fulfilled, an unquenchable need. Now, this is important in two different ways. First, if you are not hungry for this elusive and ultimately mysterious art called true acting, you will not be able to hold on, for the work ahead of you is enormous. It is demanding in ways that you cannot yet imagine. And the hard work never ends. Never.

What I am asking you to do is to really take a look at what you are actually hungry for. It is very easy to walk around saying "I want to be an actor. I want to be an actor." Lots of people talk this particular talk. But what does that mean? And what does that mean to you if you say it? What drives you, what makes you get out of bed every morning and lead the specific life you lead every day?

There is another way the word *hunger* is important to actors. Only by understanding hunger, personally and intimately, can we begin to relate in an authentic way, a human way, to the words of the play we will ultimately have to inject life into. I am saying that every character in every well-written play is also hungry. They are hungry to achieve something, to accomplish something, to fight for what they believe to be as right and necessary as water and air.

By the way, I want you to be very clear on something. Every single thing I say to you is the absolute truth. Does that sound arrogant? It's not. I am talking to you like an actor. I am telling you that every word I say here is the truth from my point of view. Now, you may disagree with me. That's OK. You see, I am making you a promise that I will always speak with you from my own truthful point of view. That is a crucial element of acting. So I am going to say it again: As an actor, I must continually fight with my life to hold on to what I know is true.

 I want you to take some time right now to open your journal again and write down your response to these two questions. Please do this before you read on.

1. What is acting?

_____

_____

2. What are the elements of great acting?

_____

_____

Acting from the Inside Out

Let's discuss the first question. You know, many people have a great misconception about what acting is. And I am not only talking about the general public, I am talking about many actors as well. I'll ask you this: Do you consider acting to be putting on masks? Do you think that playing a part in a play is, in some way, putting on a mask to become the character?

I say no, it's not. In fact, great acting is always a taking off of masks, layer after layer. Rather than putting on a mask to become the character, you must continually unmask yourself to reveal the character.

Who is the character? You are. Aren't you? Whose voice is speaking the words? Your voice. Whose feet carry your body around the stage? Your feet. Whose heart is pounding before you make your first entrance? Your heart. The character is always you. You cannot escape this simple truth, so you may as well embrace it. And if any acting teacher tries to make you feel like you must be less of who you really are to do the part, or makes you feel bad in any way for being who you really are, run in the other direction as fast as you can. I hope you will find a teacher who will help and encourage you to always be more who you truly are.

> I tore myself away from the safe comfort of certainties through my love for truth — and truth rewarded me.
> Simone de Beauvoir

Many people think that acting is something that is contained in the personality of the actor. You know, like if Sally is the life of the party, Sally would make a good actor. The truth is, as you may already know, acting is a craft. And to learn this craft takes a huge commitment, consistent attention, and time. Musicians, dancers, athletes—all performers—know that to improve their skills, they must spend hours every day working at it. Rarely do actors think this way. A pianist will play scales day after day after day so that ultimately the scales will disappear and all that remains is the musician in the music. And that's what I hope you are after as an acting student. To work on exercise after exercise after exercise, day after day after day, so that ultimately all the work drops away and what is left is you in your acting.

What does that mean, "you in your acting"? I'll answer that with another question. Do you really want to be the next great Johnny Depp? Forget about it. We already have a great Johnny Depp. Acting is not an imitative art form. No true art is. So, if you are in any way trying to be a Johnny Depp or a Claire Danes (or any other actor whose work you admire), you are headed down a path to certain disaster. Oh yes, you may make some money at it, but your work will always be hollow and so will your heart.

So if acting is not an imitation of something, and it is not an illustration of something, what is it?

The Key to the Highway

True acting is an act of creation. This is very important.

Think about it this way. To me, the most awesome act of creation is having a baby. I have two children, so I have been blessed to experience this personally. Now, we all know the facts of how a baby is made. We know all about the sperm meets the egg and so on. We have photographs of every stage of the embryo's growth, and doctors can tell us countless intricate and technical details about the minute-by-minute development of the baby inside the mother's womb. But not one doctor, not one scientist anywhere on this planet, can tell us a single thing about the most essential part of this act of creation. They cannot tell us anything about life itself. Where does it come from? How does it come to us? It is absolutely unexplainable, isn't it? It is a most extraordinary mystery, this thing called life.

> Falsehood is easy, truth so difficult.
> T. S. Eliot

Acting, which is absolutely about the act of injecting life into that which is without life, is also a mystery. You pick up the script and you look at the words given to you by the playwright. Words that, if he or she is a great playwright, were forged from an original spark of life. Now, what is your job? Your job is to inhabit those words and breathe life into them, to bring them to life. With whose life? With your life.

So, if great acting is an act of creation, there are certain skills we must strengthen so that we are strong, willing, and able to allow that which is unexplainable to occur. Notice how carefully that sentence is worded. Read it again:

We must be strong, willing, and able to allow that which is unexplainable to occur.

You cannot make life onstage happen any more than you can "make" a baby have life. A mother can do all the hundreds of things that are recommended to take care of herself while she's pregnant. A doctor can use the powerful tools of medical science to ensure that the growth of the unborn child will go as well as possible. But the life part, well, that's a gift. It is the part that is totally out of our control. The same with acting.

But even if we can't make it happen, there are things we can do so that the "growth" of our life onstage will go as well as possible. This is the craft part. This is where we must work on developing in ourselves the fundamental skills of true acting, and these are the things I will explore with you more specifically as we continue to work together. Right now, I want to introduce you to four fundamental skills so that you have time to think about them before we begin further investigation.

> In my experience, there is only one motivation, and that is desire. No reasons or principle contain it or stand against it.
> Jane Smiley

1. Full-body listening and availability.

True acting is not a "me, myself, and I" form of art. It is one that finds its source in our moment-to-moment relationship with our partners onstage and with everything in our environment.

2. Being in the present.

The past is over and dead. The future is pure fantasy. Yet if we are honest with ourselves, we begin to see that we spend most of our time caught up in either going over and over the past or attempting to predict, map out, and control the future. The truth is that life, and being alive, only exists in this moment right now.

3. Really doing what you're doing.

The basis of all true acting is the reality of doing. When we do something, we really do it. We don't pretend and we don't fake. This means that rather than making it look like we are doing something, we are, in each moment, actually doing what we are doing. Sounds simple, but this is a profound idea that affects every aspect of our craft.

4. Becoming instinctively and spontaneously responsive.

As infants, we expressed ourselves fully, freely, and without fearing what people thought about us. Then, as we grew up, we worked very hard at being liked and winning approval. This powerful desire caused us to limit and censor how we really felt, what we really thought, who we truly were. True acting demands that we relearn and reclaim our ability to be exactly who we are and that we rediscover our true voice.

chapter 2

Approaching the Play

It's really very simple. If you are going to act, you have to be able to read the play like an actor.

Think of it this way. Edna the cab driver can read a play and tell you the story line. She can read the script and speak about the circumstances the characters are involved in. Also, in a literal and very basic way, Edna can tell you what the characters want.

But you're not Edna the cabdriver, you are an actor, and you have to be able to "see" a world of things going on in the play that Edna can't see. I am saying that as an actor you must strengthen in yourself a deeper sensitivity to the play. One of my teachers used to say that the actor has to be able to X-ray the script.

It's just like Dr. Kowal the chiropractor. You and I can look at an X-ray and say, "Oh yes, that's the spine and those are the bones." But Dr. Kowal, honed by massive amounts of hard work on his craft, has developed a greater sensitivity to the X-ray. He can look at the same X-ray that we looked at, but he will see all kinds of subtleties in the formation of the spine that you and I are totally blind to. Dr. Kowal can tell you all kinds of things about the condition of that person's life. He can also speak about the root causes of the pain that brought the patient to his office to end their suffering.

Your Full Attention Is Required

To give you a new and useful way to look at the plays you will be working on, I am going to introduce three major dramatic components. And to introduce these elements, here is a fundamental acting truth: If you want to be a better actor, first be a better person.

One more time so you know this is a crucial point I am making: *If you want to be a better actor, first be a better person.* Say these words to yourself and see what feelings it arouses.

If I want to be a better actor, first I must be a better person.

Go ahead, close your eyes and let those words wash over your insides for a few minutes, then continue reading.

When I say those words to myself, I immediately get the feeling that acting is not just about me. These words impress on me that being a good actor has to do with my relationship to the world around me. These words also suggest to me that being a good actor has to do with my relationship with the people I care about and the difference I make by the things I choose to do in this life. These simple words expand my notion of acting and raise it to a truly spiritual level.

Have you ever thought of acting in this way? It isn't talked about very much, but when you begin to explore this notion, you will see that it is absolutely the only path toward true satisfaction, longevity, and an unceasing passion for this most beautiful and elusive art.

I said it, so now I really have to define it. What do I mean by being a better person? To answer this question, I am going to break things down into three pieces. The three pieces are desire, the opponent, and suffering. Let's call these the "ABC of acting and life." These three items we are about to discuss—desire, the opponent, and suffering—are not only the three major truths of our lives, they are also the keys to understanding every script you will read for the rest of your life. This makes sense because if the craft of acting does not relate to our lives and how we operate as human beings, it is false.

The ABC of acting and life. Here we go.

A. Desire: *What Gets You Out of Bed Each Morning?*

I have a new distinction for you. It is not that we have desire, and we do have desire, it is that *we are desire*.

> Desire is the very essence of man.
>
> *Baruch Spinoza*

Listen to this very carefully:

It is not that we have desire, and we do have desire, it is that we are desire.

✒ This may sound a little odd to you but I want you to give it some thought. What might I mean by the statement **we are desire**? Why don't you write some reactions to this statement in your journal.

_____
_____
_____
_____
_____
_____
_____
_____

Yes, the fact is that *we are* desire. What got Mommy and Daddy together in the first place? Desire. You know that fateful day at the grocery store when Daddy got his first look at your mom, dropped the tomatoes, and said to himself, "Wow!" And Mommy got her first look back at your dad, dropped the lettuce, and said to herself, "Wow!" Suddenly, Mommy and Daddy were together making a beautiful salad! And what do you think led to their first kiss? Desire. And then, of course we get to you! You began in the midst of some real strong desire don't you think?

> It is the nature of desire not to be satisfied, and most men live only for the gratification of it.
> *Aristotle*

Of course if we look at the story of the sperm and the egg, we are looking at the clearest factual and scientific evidence that we "are" desire. I know you have studied the details of this epic story in school. Out of millions, how many sperm fulfill their ultimate quest? Yes, one. And that's no easy journey the sperm sets out on. The environment it finds itself in has huge obstacles in store. But does that determined little guy cave in to these pressures? *No!*

So, you see, on a cellular level, you and I, all of us, are desire, and we cannot elude the power of its force on our lives. Some people try to evade desire. What about the person who commits himself to giving up all desire and goes seeking a guru on a mountaintop? Hasn't he merely adopted the desire to have no desire? The answer, of course, is yes. You see? More desire!

If you stop to examine it, you will find that behind every choice you make, underneath every word you speak, inside every thought you think, fueling every fantasy you imagine, and even infiltrating your dreams at night is desire! It's there in the things that run around in your mind before you fall asleep at night, and it's there in the morning when you awake, driving you out of your bed. (Along with having to go to the bathroom.)

Why is this so incredibly important to come to terms with? Why is it so vital to see the effects of desire in your own life? It is important because every character you will ever play is also a human being who is living with a specific and unquenchable desire. So, ultimately, if you cannot understand the desire of the character in both a human and deeply personal way, you cannot play the part.

> When I hear somebody sigh, "Life is hard," I am always tempted to ask, "Compared to what?"
> Sydney J. Harris

B. The Opponent: *No One Said It Was Going to Be Easy*

As soon as there is desire, there will be a force that opposes that desire. This is always true, always. I call this force "the opponent."

You can count on the fact that the opponent will be present to make it more difficult to accomplish the things you desire. You may not prefer it, like it, or believe it, but when you look at life with eyes really open, you see that this is simply the way life is built.

> In your journal, write about what gets in the way of you fulfilling the things you most desire. After your journal work, come back to this chapter.

_____
_____
_____
_____
_____
_____
_____

To get more specific now, there are two types of opponents we are faced with: the external opponent and the internal opponent. (As we discuss this, see if the writing you did in your journal links up with these descriptions.)

The External Opponent

Every day, just as with you and me, all people go about their lives with their own deeply held desires. Sometimes, an outside force will step in and either make fulfilling that desire very challenging or this force will attempt to wipe out the desire all together.

Here's a simple example of an external opponent.

> Shelley has just moved to town. She is sixteen and in tenth grade. After two months of school, Shelley has had a difficult time making friends, but last week, something wonderful happened. Shelley was invited by Carol to hang out at Carol's house after school.
>
> Carol and Shelley had a great time during that first visit, and they began to get together every day after school to do homework together. On a few of those days, Carol's best friend Stacey also came over. Stacey has not said anything to Carol, but she is very jealous, and she is not happy that Carol has been spending time with Shelley.
>
> Today, Stacey told a lie to Carol. She told Carol that she heard Shelley talking to another kid at school, and that Shelley told this kid that Carol lives in a "crumb of a house"! Stacey knows that Carol, who lives in a very modest house with her mom, dad, and younger brother, has always been intimidated by the kids at school who live in big houses.
>
> Carol was very upset to hear that Shelley had betrayed their new friendship. So, although they were supposed to get together again today, Carol just told Shelley that she had to cancel the homework session for today and that she is going to be too busy to get together next week as well.

My question for you is: Who is the external opponent in this little story? And what desires did the opponent step in to destroy?

If you said that Stacey is the external opponent, you are correct. Do you see how both Carol and Shelley had very simple desires that brought them together and how Stacey stepped in to wipe these desires out?

What were the desires Stacey could not tolerate? Shelley had the deep desire to make a friend in her new school. Carol also had a desire to make a new friend and to be with someone who was fun to hang out with. But Stacey, acting out of fear and with a mean, self-serving, and selfish attitude, wreaked havoc on the new bond forming between Shelley and Carol. She also caused a lot of pain, right? Yes, the external opponent always causes pain.

The Truth Reflected in Every Arena

Here is an interesting example to highlight the basic truth of the force called the opponent. It's called sports. Obvious, right? Yes, all sports were created to have a specific desire and an opponent who makes the desire more difficult to accomplish. And who created sports? People did. People created sports as a reflection of the truth of our lives, and they intensified this truth and raised the stakes. Hey, that's just like theater!

Let's look at football for a moment. If you are on the New York Jets and you have the ball at your own five-yard line, how many yards do you need to go to get a touchdown? Yes, you need to go another ninety-five yards. Isn't your desire to get a touchdown? Yes, it is. So, with the football on your own five-yard line, will the other team, the Miami Dolphins, your opponent, try to stop you from making progress in your effort? Yes, they will.

Now, imagine that you have moved the ball forward ninety yards, and you are on the Dolphin's five-yard line, so now you only have to go five yards to score the touchdown. My question is, here on the five-yard line, will the Dolphins' defense get less intense or more intense? Yes, *more intense*! And this is how the opponent operates in our lives as well. The closer we get to fulfilling our desire, the more fierce the opponent will become.

> Nobody knows what you want except you. And nobody will be as sorry as you if you don't get it. Wanting some other way to live is proof enough of deserving it. Having it is hard work, but not having it is sheer hell.
> —Lillian Hellman

Of course, you will also find this life truth in every great movie or play.

🪶 In your journal, consider and write about *Lord of the Rings*. When Frodo takes on the mission of the ring, what is his desire? Does he face any opponents? Who are they? Does Frodo suffer? How about Romeo and Juliet? What is the desire of the young lovers? Who are the opponents? Do Romeo and Juliet suffer?

_____

_____

_____

🪶 Here are some more writing assignments for your journal work. First, I want you to write about examples of the external opponent from history. What events have you studied that are clear instances of the external opponent, in his lust for power, destroying the desires of other people in the world?

Next, please write about times when you have encountered the external opponent in your own life. Get specific. What was your desire and how did the opponent try to sabotage it? Did that person succeed? Did this cause you pain?

Then identify times in your life when you may have done something that made you the external opponent in someone else's life and you caused him or her pain. It might be as simple as a time when your little brother wanted that last chocolate chip cookie, and you took it out of his hand and ate it yourself.

Go ahead and write and see what you come up with: when you have had an external opponent squashing your desire and when you have been the external opponent to someone else.

_____

_____

_____

_____

_____

_____

_____

The Internal Opponent

The truth is that we often create our own obstacles to fulfilling our deepest desires. Do you know about Ed the construction worker who had a peanut butter and jelly sandwich for lunch every day?

> Every day, when the horn blew at noon, Ed would sit with the other guys on the crew, open his lunch box, and pull out a sandwich. As he unwrapped the sandwich and saw that it was peanut butter and jelly, Ed would cry out, "I hate peanut butter and jelly sandwiches!" This went on for months and months. Every single day, Ed would open his lunch box, pull out his sandwich, unwrap it, see the peanut butter and jelly, and cry, "I hate peanut butter and jelly sandwiches!" Finally, Bob, who sat next to Ed every day, asked, "Man! Why don't you tell your wife to make you a different sandwich!" Ed shot back, "What wife? I'm single, I make my own sandwiches!"

Who's Listening to Whom?

To begin to make clear to you the internal opponent, here's a question: Have you ever had the experience, maybe late at night when you are in your room by yourself, of your mind being flooded with unpleasant thoughts? And, no matter what you do, the thoughts will not stop? Maybe the thoughts sound like this: "What's the matter with me?" "I'm not good enough!" "I'll never be as good as so-and-so!" "I'm just too dumb to ever succeed!"—and on and on.

I have asked this same question to groups I have worked with in every part of the world, all across Europe, South America, Canada, and the United States. In every group, no matter what language they speak, every hand in the room goes up saying, "Yes, I have these kinds of thoughts." Isn't that interesting? Isn't it interesting that people all around the world are having the same, uncontrollable self-critical thoughts as you?

Well, if that's the case, then let's suppose for a moment that the thoughts aren't even your own. Let's imagine that there is a radio station with a powerful transmitter and a very tall antenna. Let's imagine that, instead of the thoughts coming from your own mind, this radio station is pumping out all these negative thoughts, and you have simply tuned in to this station. You didn't mean to tune in, but somehow, you, and every other person all around the world, did tune in, and all of you are pulling in these negative thoughts from the air waves!

Here's my next question: Does an infant have these kinds of negative, self-critical thoughts? If you are an infant and your mommy is pushing you in your stroller and another baby goes by in her stroller and she is wearing expensive diapers, do you think that you would have a thought like, "Hey! That baby has the good diapers! Why didn't my mommy get me the good diapers? This sucks! I knew it, my mommy really doesn't love me!" Or if the other baby going by had curly hair, do you think you would have thoughts like, "Why didn't I get curly hair! My hair is straight. I am so plain, no one will ever like me!" Do you think a little baby has these kinds of thoughts? Obviously not, right?

So, if you did not have these thoughts when you were born, when did you tune in to the "critical thought radio station"? Was it when you started to go to school? Was it when your parents first scolded you? Was it when you first began to play with other kids and you compared yourself to them? Well, scientists have some ideas about all this, but the truth is that we don't really know precisely when these negative thoughts begin to take control of the mind. The important thing to note is that this new awareness has to do with attention.

Careful! The Mirror Is a Trap

Here's a simple question: When you are listening to the thoughts in your mind, where is your attention? Is it directed out toward the world around you or is it directed inward toward yourself? Obviously, if you are listening to the thinking in your head, your attention is directed at yourself. This means that during those periods when you are absorbed in negative thinking, you are no longer available to the world around you. This is a problem in two main respects: First, life and aliveness is only accessible to us when we are in a relationship with the world around us in the present moment. Second, when your attention is more on yourself than on what is happening around you, you are in danger! I am sure you have heard the phrase "lost in thought"?

Here's a story about the danger of being lost in thought. One day, when I was very young and living in New York City, I was on the corner of 57th Street and Ninth Avenue at 7 a.m., waiting for a bus. I was eating a banana, and I was lost in thought. Did you ever see in the cartoons a moment where the cartoon character gets hit in the head and he sees stars? Well, I was eating my banana, lost in thought, and suddenly something hit me so hard on my forehead that I literally saw stars! I went reeling back, but I stayed on my feet. When my eyes finally opened, I saw a crazy-looking man with wild, knotted hair about twenty feet away from me holding a two-by-four piece of lumber and waving it in the air. He had just bashed me in the head with that big piece of wood! I remember the two of us, the

SHELTER	MUSIC Teacher	Kyle RANKIN, DIR LA
Adventures of Rufus the Fantastic Pet	Grandmother	Ryan Bellgardt, Producer/Director LA
On the Other Side*	TALENT Ticket Agent	Coullias-blanc, Dir NYC
Lone Star Justice ID TV	Ticket Seller	Jarrett Creative; Dir Jonny Mars TX
PepsiCo	Principal	M Luem, Dir - Above Average Prod NYC
Met Life	Principal	VanDusen, DIr - MacGuffin Films NYC
Home Depot	Principal	Carat USA NYC
University of Texas	Principal	Sam Schachter, Director - DHD Films, Dallas
Big Y Foods Inc.	Principal	Trio Films Productions LA
AMGEN	Principal	John Higgins, Producer - The Station NYC
Live Your Best Life Now	Principal	Lichtenstein, 4C2 Creative-Lightstone NYC
Pfizer Inc	Principal	DelPhi Productions NYC
Voice America Women's Network	Principal	VAWN
SANOFI	Principal	J Andres, DIr. - Block Prod NYC
MERCK	Principal	Harrison and Star LLC NYC
MERCK	Principal	DDB NYC
The New York Times Magazine	Principal	Editorial, Katherine Wolkoff NYC
Solstice Health	Principal	Jeff Morgan Studio NYC
Century 21 Department Store	Principal	Production Farm NYC
Uncommon Women and Others	Mrs. Plub	Mad 'n' Merry Theatre NYC
Leviticus in Love	Mother	Corozine Studio Theatre NYC
Complicated	Psychiatrist	Corozine Studio Theatre NYC
A Reunion of Sorts	Girlfriend	McKinney TX Rep Theatre
Belles, The Reunion*	Older Sister	McKinney TX Rep Theatre

Acting: Joan See, Dir NY Conservatory Dramatic Arts; Matthew Corozine Studio, Meisner NYC; Inside Game, Michelle & Robert Colt NYC; Robert Colt Art of Not Acting Studio NYC
Commercial: Don Case Casting NYC; House Casting NYC; Trey Lawson, CD NBC NYC; Amy Gossels, CD NYC
Voiceover: Robin Miles, VOXPERTISE, NYC
Improv: Barry Shapiro, CD Herman & Lipson Casting NYC; The ALternative Comedy Theatre DFW; CD Kevin Howard, Dallas Actors Group

*On the Other Side p- Cannes Film Festival Winner
*Belles, The Reunion - Winner Peoples' Choice Best Actress

crazy man and I, staring at each other. He looked like he was going to come at me again with that two-by-four at any moment. And then, just as suddenly as I was hit, the guy turned and ran off and disappeared into the traffic. At the same time, my bus pulled up. I climbed up the stairs of the bus, dropped in some money, sat in an empty seat, and finished eating my banana—which was still in my hand!

For months after that incident, I suffered from a severe concussion and all the symptoms that go with it. What a wake-up call, don't you think? It was a big lesson in the importance of being awake and the danger of walking through life lost in thought!

Now, let's talk about babies again. Have you been around them much? Where do they always have their attention? Yes, at all times, babies have their attention directed out toward the world. When you play with a baby, or make silly faces at her, you know that her total attention is on you. I think this is one reason why almost everyone in the world loves being with babies. They remind us that we are human beings. (And this is exactly what great theater offers. Great theater, which is rare, reminds audience members that they are human.)

Then the baby grows up and unfortunately, like most people, puts a mirror up in front of her face. Think about this for a moment. I just said that most people in this world are walking around with a mirror up in front of their faces. For these people, their attention goes out toward the mirror and bounces back onto themselves. And with their attention on themselves, the self-critical and negative thinking gets more intense. That radio station we discussed earlier gets louder and louder. "What do people think about me?" "How do I look?" "No one will ever love me!"

> This is, in fact, the internal opponent, and just like the external opponent, the internal opponent causes great suffering! Have you experienced this yourself? Write about this in your journal.

_____
_____
_____
_____
_____
_____
_____

Here's the good news! First, because you were once a baby, you already have the ability to live without listening to the radio station, but it will take some work to retrain yourself. It is, in fact, the Meisner Approach that offers the best and only way I have ever found to reawaken and strengthen your innate ability to have your attention directed fully outward toward the world so that you are no longer plagued by the control mechanisms of the mind. What a relief! And we will start to explore these methods in the following chapters. But first, let's look at the third part of the ABC of acting and life.

C. Suffering: *The Joy in the Struggle*

This one is easy, and it really needs little explanation. You and I, all of us, know suffering. Whether the suffering has been caused by an external or internal opponent, we have experienced pain and great difficulties. We are talking about the pain that always accompanies our attempt to fulfill our deepest desires.

> *Every problem has a gift for you in its hands.*
> — Johannes Bach

Here is something to take careful note of: Suffering is part of the plan, and it was given to us with great purpose. Think about these two scenarios.

Scenario one: Your mission is to climb Mount Everest, the highest mountain on earth, and you must do it alone, without supplemental oxygen and in the winter season. Also, you must beat the climbing record held by Christian Stengl, who did the climb in sixteen hours and forty-two minutes. You will have three years to train so that you are prepared to handle the many dangers of the climb such as altitude sickness, weather, and wind.

Scenario two: Your mission is to climb up a staircase in a two-story house we have chosen in Westport, Connecticut. The stairs are carpeted and there is a handrail to hold onto. You must make the climb without supplemental oxygen, but you can certainly eat a good breakfast first. We will fly you to Hartford airport. Our limo will pick you up there and take you to the front door of the house. A butler will escort you from the front door to the staircase. You have one week to train for this task.

Let's say that you have now successfully completed both your missions. Wow. Congratulations!

The Gifts of the Challenge

First, I want you to go back in your mind and relive the climb up Mount Everest. Remember how you fell, bruised your leg, and thought you would have to turn back? But when you stopped the bleeding and bandaged yourself up, you kept going forward, scaling the mountain, step by step. Reflect on the mistake you made with the backpack, losing half your water supply and putting your life in jeopardy. Think about the difficulty of breathing the closer you got to your goal and how dizzy and faint you became. And now remember, after shaking with the fear that you had lost your way and starting to believe that you would not live through this ordeal, the heavy fog began to clear and you turned to see the peak just yards away.

Now reexperience in your mind the exact moment you actually stepped onto the peak and scraped the ice away from the face of your watch and realized that you had made the climb in sixteen hours and twenty-nine minutes. You did it! Well, in your imagination anyway. And in your imagination, what do you think the feelings would be at the moment of your incredible accomplishment after the great suffering you experienced on your ascent of Mount Everest and after three years of intensive, exhausting training and planning? Might joy come to mind? How about a profound sense of joy?

> He who knows no hardships will know no hardihood. He who faces no calamity will need no courage. Mysterious though it is, the characteristics in human nature which we love best grow in a soil with a strong mixture of troubles.
>
> *Harry Emerson Fosdick*

Now I want you to imagine your other task, climbing the set of stairs in the Westport, Connecticut, house. Remember looking at the stairs and thinking that this is a piece of cake. Reflect on the casual way you took each step and how effortless it was. And now relive the moment you reached the top of the stairs. Well, how do you imagine you felt at the moment of achieving this particular goal? Was there a profound sense of joy in this accomplishment? Of course not, right? Why do you think there is not much joy?

These examples make very clear that to the extent things are difficult and we move through these challenges with an unceasing commitment, we will experience the other side of the suffering, which is joy. This is a truth that we often forget when things get tough. We may wish things were less difficult and we may try to avoid all difficulties, but the truth remains that the only path to deep satisfaction is by sticking with our promise even though the path gets hard. And it is, in fact, the suffering that makes the joy possible.

> In this age, which believes that there is a short cut to everything, the greatest lesson to be learned is that the most difficult way is, in the long run, the easiest.
> *Henry Miller*

It is easy to see all around us people who never commit to anything. When things become uncomfortable, most people run in the other direction. They drop one commitment and find another—and another and another. Sadly, the people who break their commitments never discover the joy that is right there waiting for them when the fog clears away.

So there you have it, the ABC of acting and life. You now have a way to think about your life, and you also have a way to look at every character in every script. Every play is the story of desire, the opponent, and suffering. And sometimes the character will discover that joy is indeed waiting on the other side. Just like Frodo!

chapter 3

Want Your House to Last? Build a Strong Foundation

In chapter 1, I told you that true acting is not a "me, myself, and I" form of art. True acting, I explained, depends on our moment-to-moment relationship with our partners onstage and with everything in our environment. I called it *full-body listening and availability*.

Today I want to work with you on what I consider to be the foundation of true acting: really listening and really talking. Let's focus on the "really listening" part first.

 I want you to try a little experiment. Before reading this chapter, I want you to spend the next twenty-four hours noticing what it is like to listen to the people in your life, especially your family members, your close friends, and others you have day-to-day contact with. As you have conversations with others, I simply want you to notice your own experience of listening.

 When the twenty-four hours are up, get your acting journal and write down what you learned about yourself and others during the past day. How did the experiment go? Any surprises or revelations?

_____

_____

_____

_____

_____

Is Anyone at Home?

Here's a question for you: Have you ever had the experience of talking to someone and knowing that he wasn't really listening to you, that he was off in his head thinking about something else?

> All human beings are interconnected, one with all other elements in creation.
> *Henry Reed*

Everyone I have ever asked that question has immediately said yes. Maybe you experienced this phenomenon during your twenty-four-hour experiment. In fact, maybe you were the one doing the ignoring. We've all had that experience: You're talking with someone and suddenly realize—or maybe knew all along—that you are a million miles away, busy in your head thinking about what you want to eat for lunch or why you didn't buy that nice shirt you saw at the mall or what you're going to do after school or wondering how your hair looks.

We must take another look at attention and dig a little deeper. If someone is talking with you and you are thinking about other things, where is your attention? The answer is your attention is on yourself. If your attention is on yourself, who is your attention not on? That's right: It is not on the other person. So if your attention is not on the other person, who are you not available to? Right again: You are not available to the other person. And ultimately, if your attention is on yourself and you are not available to the other person, are you really "in a relationship" with that other person? No, you are not. Then who are you having a relationship with? I'll tell you: You are having a relationship with the thoughts in your head.

Sadly, many people walk through life unavailable to the people closest to them, disconnected from everyone, in real relationship with no one. Sounds kind of lonely, don't you think? Now, if people are behaving this way in real life, you can bet that a fair number of actors are doing the same thing onstage.

Have you noticed yet that I keep relating this thing called true acting to our lives?

An Actor Who Acts? No! A Human Being Who Acts

There's a reason for that. Many actors think there is some kind of separation: Over here on the right, I am an actor, and over here on the left, I am a person. That is a totally false notion. There is no separation. We must strive to bring our own humanness to our work—all that we are, from the petty, selfish, and small in us to the magnificent, generous, and wise. For theater is not an imitation of our lives; it demands a greater truth. And it is this greater truth we are grappling with together.

I have observed countless actors who are unavailable to their partners onstage, disconnected from them, in real relationship only with the thoughts in their heads—thoughts such as "Am I entertaining them?" or "I think they really like me tonight" or "Didn't I just laugh convincingly?" or "I really do have expressive eyes" or "Wait until they hear me do the speech in Act II." When your attention is on yourself, there is absolutely no possibility for true acting.

Of course, it would be absurd for me to tell you, "Just get out of your head and put your attention out there." It takes some retraining to make this fundamental acting skill habitual. And *habitual* is a great word, because if any skill is going to be useful to you, it must become like tying your shoes, like breathing—so that you're not thinking about doing it, you're doing it. The good news is that at the end of this chapter, I will give you a wonderful exercise to begin that process.

Now, let's shift our focus and examine together the "really talking" part of really listening and really talking. I am going to give you another experiment to have fun with.

👁 As you travel through your life for the next twenty-four hours, I want you to notice your first response to the people and things you come into contact with. Simply notice your very first thoughts and feelings as people, things, and events cross your path. Do not try to have thoughts and feelings about anything; simply notice the first ones you do have as you encounter whomever and whatever it is that you encounter.

For example, as you walk down the street and you notice a person approaching you, what is the very first thought that runs through your mind about that person? I won't explain this experiment fully for you, but let me say that the words **your first response** are very important. Try to bring to your awareness the very first thoughts and feelings you have, and do your best to be absolutely honest with yourself.

> When you have done this for a day, write about your experience in your journal and then you may continue with this chapter.

_____
_____
_____
_____
_____
_____

What do you think the point of this exercise was?

What Can We Actually Control in This Life?

The thing is, we all have immediate responses to everything. Often they occur so lightning fast, flashing through our minds and bodies, that we don't really notice them. Sometimes our thoughts and feelings are not the responses we would like to have, or they are not the responses that we think we should have, so when we do notice them, we push them away or deny them altogether. Certainly, we don't express them to anyone. They remain part of our secret lives.

> Pain and foolishness lead to great bliss and complete knowledge, for Eternal Wisdom created nothing under the sun in vain.
> Kahlil Gibran

Why do you think we keep to ourselves so many of the responses we have to people and the world around us? Well, on a practical level, we want to act in a manner we believe to be proper in certain social situations. For instance, you might think the admissions counselor is having a "bad hair day," but you don't say anything because you want to get into the college.

On a deeper level, we censor our responses in an attempt to control and manipulate life. We all want to be liked and feel comfortable and safe. Whether it's to hold onto a girlfriend or to keep from being cast out by a group of peers or to make our parents think we are exactly who we think they want us to be, we try to control and manipulate. This process becomes automatic and unconscious as we become adept at expressing only a small portion of what we are actually thinking and feeling.

Over the years, as we perfect and polish the way in which we express ourselves, we all develop an act in life. *Act* is a great word for it because it certainly isn't all of who we truly are, and it doesn't tell the whole story.

I am not saying that the act we develop is a bad thing—it's about survival. I always used to laugh to myself when, as a teenager, I would hear other kids describe me as "quiet and intense," as if that were all I was. I found it funny because I knew that I was all kinds of things: goofy, sensitive, silly, loud, moody, playful, and so on. But when I stopped and considered how I carried myself in life a lot of the time, I realized that "quiet and intense" was an accurate description.

Here's another example. Recently, I taught one of my Meisner workshops to a group of high school students. There was one young woman who, no matter what was happening, had an expression on her face and a posture in her body that said, "I don't really care about any of this and nothing really matters to me." I noticed the same body language when I saw her talking and hanging out with some of her classmates during the breaks. Then we did an exercise in which people bring in and talk about an object that has great importance to them, something that makes them feel uplifted and joyous. This young woman shared with the group a picture of herself when she was about three years old. I was struck by the photo and the huge, warm, and absolutely delighted smile on this toddler's face, the excitement and openness in her eyes. I wondered what had happened to this young woman that led her to adopt her own particular approach to life, her own act. I wondered why it became so critical for her to make us all think that nothing really mattered to her.

> Here's what I want you to do. Go back to your journal and write about your act in life. Write as if you were an outside observer watching yourself go through your day-to-day existence. How would you describe your behavior to someone who didn't know you? Do that now and then come back.

_____

_____

_____

_____

_____

You might be wondering how all this relates to the "really talking" part of really talking and really listening. It has to do with the difference between working from our head and working from our instinctual selves.

The Truth of the Moment Is Always Appropriate

Listen, if I suddenly threw a burning log straight at you with great force, believe me, you would have an immediate and powerful response, both physically and emotionally. You wouldn't stop to think about how to respond to the burning log coming at your face—you'd respond to it. Isn't that true? I mean, do you think you would pause to say to yourself, "If I hit the log with the back of my hand in this clever way, that girl over there will think I am really manly and attractive and will want to go out with me." Pretty silly, right?

> Relationships are all there is. Everything in the universe only exists because it is in relationship to everything else. Nothing exists in isolation. We have to stop pretending we are individuals that can go it alone.
>
> Margaret Wheatley

"Being appropriate" is a useful skill in life, but it's not very helpful to us as actors. We must be willing to give up the need to be appropriate. We must shed all censoring of ourselves and all controlling of others. We have to trust that when we express our own point of view fully and truthfully, we are always "appropriate." We must open ourselves to the possibility of authentic and honest relationships that live in the present. As playwright David Mamet said so beautifully in his book *Writing in Restaurants*, the theater is one of the last places where people can behold real relationships, where the audience is reminded that authentic communication between human beings is still possible!

As I promised earlier, I'm going to conclude this chapter with an exercise that will start to make the conceptual real for you. The exercise is called Repetition, and it is the basis, or foundation, of the Meisner Approach to the craft of acting. I learned the exercise from my teacher, Sanford Meisner. Repetition is really very simple, and it grows in a series of stages.

By simple, I don't mean that it's easy; I am saying that it's uncomplicated. Right now, I am going to give you only the very first step, and I want you to practice it with a partner. In fact, before you read the directions, go find someone to work with so you can try Repetition as I teach it to you.

Repetition: Scales for the Actor

Got your partner? Good. Here's how it works:

Sit in chairs facing each other. Sit a comfortable distance apart as if you were sitting down to talk with each other.

Pick the person who will begin the exercise. The partner who begins will be Partner A.

To Partner A: Turn your head away from the other person. When you are ready, turn back and look at your partner. As you turn to your partner, say out loud to your partner the very first thing you notice about her.

The thing you say must not be any kind of assumption like, "You really don't like me." And it must not be a question like, "Why do you wear pink nail polish?" It must simply be a physical observation, and it must be the very first thing you actually notice.

So, if the first thing you noticed as you turned to your partner was the pink nail polish she has painted on her nails, you might simply say, "Pink nail polish." That's simple, isn't it? Remember, saying the very first thing you notice is key!

To Partner B: When your partner says whatever he says, I want you to repeat what you hear. So, in our example, if your partner said, "Pink nail polish," you would say what? That's right, you would say, "Pink nail polish."

Back to Partner A: You must now repeat what you hear. Your partner just said, "Pink nail polish," so you would say . . . ? Yes, that's it, "Pink nail polish." Not too tricky, right?

The two of you would then continue the repetition this way, back and forth like ping-pong, always repeating what you hear.

How do you know when to stop the repetition? Well, when it gets uncomfortable or boring or you just want to stop for any reason—keep going! When you do finally stop, let Partner B start with a new observation and repetition and do the exercise some more.

Before the next chapter, do a bunch of repetitions, and try to do it with someone who has a sincere interest in working on the exercise with you.

Repetition: A Few Pointers

The person who begins the repetition must be ruthless with him- or herself about saying the first thing he observes. If it's your turn to begin and you feel yourself observing a few different things and then choosing one of them to say, stop and start over. Why? Because this means that you "thought" about a few things you observed before you said anything.

You both must always repeat what is said, but you shouldn't attempt to repeat *how* it is said. This is not about imitating your partner or copying the quality of how he or she sounds. It is simply about hearing what you hear and repeating what you hear. Don't consciously change how it comes out of your mouth: leave it alone.

Make sure to take out all pauses as you repeat. Don't rush the exercise, but do repeat what you hear as soon as you actually hear it. This rule will keep you from thinking about the exercise because you will be fully involved in actually doing it. Also, over time, by taking out the pauses, you will be reinvigorating your innate ability to stay out of your head!

chapter 4

If You're Going to Do It, Why Not Really Do It?

Ready for some fun? Here's what I want you to do.

Go put on a pair of sneakers. When you have them on, tie the laces on one sneaker and leave the other shoe untied. Please do that now.

All set? Your next task is to find someone and ask him or her to tie several extremely tight, complicated knots into the laces that are untied. Tell this person to make knots so tight that it will be next to impossible to get them untied. Do that now—do not read on until you do—and then come back to this page for the next assignment.

Here is the assignment: Ask the person who tied the knots to get a watch or a clock and be prepared to time you for three minutes. The person should say "ready, set, go" and then tell you when each minute goes by: "Two minutes left. One minute left." At one minute, your timekeeper must announce every ten-second point: "Fifty seconds. Forty seconds. Thirty seconds." When the three minutes are up, the person should say stop.

The directions for your part are simple: Using only your fingers, you must get all the knots out in three minutes.

Do not continue on with this chapter until you have completed the three-minute untie-the-knot-a-thon. When the three minutes are up, go immediately to the next page.

OK, I'd like you to get out your acting journal and write about what you experienced while you attempted to untie the knots. What did you think and feel as you did it? Do that now and then we'll talk about it.

_____
_____
_____
_____
_____
_____

What Are You Really Doing?

My first question to you is: Did you do it? I'm not asking if you got all the knots out in three minutes. I'm asking did you really try to untie the knots? Or did you try to make it look like you were really trying to get the knots out?

> Conquering any difficulty always gives one a secret joy, for it means pushing back a boundary-line and adding to one's liberty.
> — Henri-Frédéric Amiel

If your answer is, "Yes, I was really trying to get the knots out," I imagine you had some responses to that effort. Maybe you got frustrated, annoyed, or angry with me for making you do this stupid thing in the first place. Maybe the task seemed so impossible it made you giggle or want to give up, or maybe you suddenly got a knot out—or all the knots out—and you were elated.

The point I am making here is that as you really tried to do something that was difficult to accomplish, you had authentic emotional responses that were beyond your control. I call this phenomenon "coming to life," and it is an essential element of true acting. You came to life while your attention was on the laces and the knots—not because you were trying to have some kind of emotional response but because you were fully invested in the task at hand.

I alluded to another aspect of true acting when I said that I was not asking if you got all the knots out. For actors, it is never about the results; it is always about the attempt. So long as you throw yourself into trying to accomplish whatever it is you must accomplish onstage, you will have the audience's full attention, whether you manage to achieve the goals or not.

I was very fortunate to play the part of Teach in a production of David Mamet's greatest play, *American Buffalo*, in Seattle. On its surface, *American Buffalo* is about three guys in a junk shop planning a robbery. As Teach, I had the two-hour ride of my life, making attempt after attempt after attempt to win a larger share in the heist, which ultimately never comes about.

How Fully Are You Doing What You Are Doing?

If drama was only about the results, audiences would have very little patience with a play like *American Buffalo*—or any great play, for that matter. We don't go to see Hamlet in hopes that maybe this time the kid will pull himself together and just kill his uncle as soon as he gets the chance. I repeat: It is never about the result; it is always about the attempt. Isn't this true in life as well?

On September 8, 1998, Mark McGwire hit home run number sixty-two and broke the season home-run record set in 1961 by Roger Maris. As McGwire closed in on that magic number, the nation's interest intensified. TV and radio stations would cut away to report on his efforts each time he stepped up to the plate, and at the stadiums, thousands upon thousands of spectators were on their feet screaming and cheering with his every swing of the bat.

What if? Imagine, just for a moment, that McGwire hit a slump after his sixty-first home run. (You'll have to imagine that his friend and rival for the record, Sammy Sosa, suffered the same fate at around fifty-nine.) And imagine that McGwire is now at the plate for his final at-bat of the season. He just swung the bat two times and missed. With two strikes against him, he has one final chance to swing at the ball—one final chance in his magical and thrilling year to break the home-run record that has challenged the game's top sluggers for the last thirty-seven years.

Picture Mark McGuire, his face sweating as he lifts his bat one more time. Watch the pitcher carefully place his fingers around the ball as he receives the final signal from the catcher. See the fans in the stadium, on their feet and afraid to breathe, and the millions of people sitting on the edge of their seats in front of their TV sets. Imagine the intensity of this moment. Here's the windup ... the pitch ... McGwire swings ...

In a few seconds, the millions of viewers will know whether McGwire has achieved his goal. But what matters right now—and what has kept fans riveted for weeks on end—is the attempt!

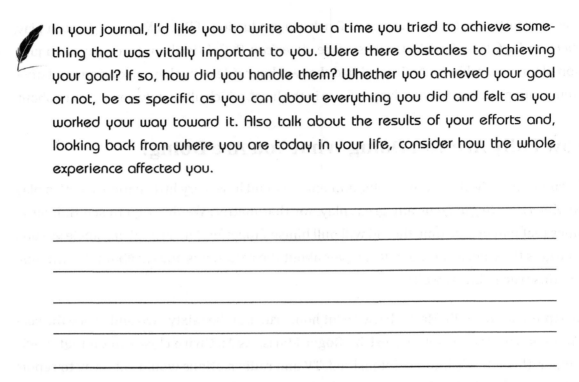

In your journal, I'd like you to write about a time you tried to achieve something that was vitally important to you. Were there obstacles to achieving your goal? If so, how did you handle them? Whether you achieved your goal or not, be as specific as you can about everything you did and felt as you worked your way toward it. Also talk about the results of your efforts and, looking back from where you are today in your life, consider how the whole experience affected you.

_____
_____
_____
_____
_____

Let's reflect back on our three-minute knot game. At any time during the three minutes, did you think that the task was simply impossible and you should give up? If so, what did you decide to do at that pivotal moment? Did you stop or did you continue trying to untie the knots?

Here are some words to remember:

Acting is doing.

It is not "talking about." It is not "feeling about," and it is not "thinking about." Sandy Meisner taught me that the basis of all true acting is the reality of *doing*. That's what this chapter is all about. When you do something, you really do it—you don't pretend to do it and you don't fake doing it.

Great acting is also about how fully you bring yourself to the doing of what you are doing. So even though something might be difficult or nearly impossible, it is your job to commit to the attempt to do it. You must leap in and make the complete attempt. To give 100 percent of yourself even though you might have no idea how to go about achieving it. As you do it, you'll discover how to do it, and that's where the life is, the life is in the doing of it!

It's important for actors to understand that although we may try to control everything in our environment, including the people around us, there is only one thing in life that we have any control over. Do you know what that is?

The truth is, although we might think we know how others will respond to the things we do or how we ourselves will feel about the things we decide to do, and though we put a lot of energy into trying to make others have the responses we would like them to have, it is all out of our control.

We can only control one thing: What we do. In terms of where you might want to start putting your attention, this is very important information both for your life and for the life in your acting, don't you think?

The Character Is Always You, and That's the Good News!

I also want to know, if you really made the attempt to untie the knots in our little three-minute game, who were you when you did the untying? Did you do it as Sherlock Holmes? As a Spice Girl? Did you try to undo the knots as Leonardo DiCaprio? Or was that *you* trying to get those knots out? Was that *you* doing this task as yourself?

Silly question? Maybe not. Although I'd be willing to bet that you tried to untie the laces as yourself rather than as some character you've seen in a play or a movie, many actors are continually performing the clichés of how they think their character would do something. In doing so, they neatly and safely detach themselves from their acting, and they whittle down the infinite possibilities of human behavior, arriving at that which has already been done and which is now lifeless.

If you are playing the part of the sister, do you have to act "sisterly"? What does that mean? Do all sisters act the same? Of course not. Some sisters become the best of friends, and some sisters are always looking for an opportunity to stab each other in the back. Isn't that true?

The thing is, when you really do what you are doing, you are forced to be fully present—and the present is the only place where life is available to us. If our job as actors is to bring life to the stage, then "really doing" is not merely important; it is fundamental. It is the key to making unique and human discoveries in our work. When you really do what you are doing, this particular thing you are involved in has never been done or experienced in precisely this way before; this moment is truly a first. Isn't that exciting? I think so.

Continuing with Repetition

In the previous chapter, I gave you an exercise to work on: Repetition. For those of you who have been practicing Repetition, I have a few questions.

As you did Repetition, did the phrase you started with ever change in any way? For instance, you might have been repeating "big shoes" back and forth, and suddenly you heard your partner say "pig shoes." So what would you then have to say? You would have to say "pig shoes." Why? Because the rule is to always repeat what you hear.

You might feel an urge to try to get the exercise back on track by correcting your partner's mistake and saying "big shoes," even though what you just heard was "pig shoes." But with Repetition there is no track. Again, your job is simply to repeat what you hear.

Another question: Did you experience any emotional response to the exercise? Did you laugh or get bored or feel frustrated? If you started to laugh, how did you handle that?

If you tried to keep from laughing in order to do the exercise right, you were not doing the exercise right. This is very important: As you repeat, I want you to allow yourself to experience any emotions that occur. If you start to laugh, allow yourself to laugh and keep repeating. If you get bored, be bored and keep repeating.

What we are doing here is taking this whole big thing we call acting and boiling it down to its very core. Repetition forces you and your partner to really listen to each other—a primary acting skill. If you are really listening to your partner, your attention is not on yourself. You begin to respond in ways that are out of your own control. You—not the you that you would like to be or the you others tell you to be, but the authentic you—comes alive in ways that will surprise you.

My "big shoes/pig shoes" example points to another basic acting concept: True acting is about working with what is really happening rather than trying to make everything into what you think should be happening

This is a big one, friends. True acting means always embracing and responding to exactly what is there at any given moment. Here, at this basic level in Repetition, it means to repeat what you hear. The exercise strengthens your ability to work immediately and spontaneously with whatever comes your way onstage. And I'll tell you, in every moment there's a lot coming your way.

As you keep working on Repetition, your senses, your availability to your partners, and your emotional responsiveness wake up in wonderful new ways.

💬 To conclude this chapter, I am going to give you the next step in Repetition. Continue to work the same way you have been working with one addition. Last time, you were starting with the first thing you observed. For example, you might say, "red sweater."

Now, beginning the same way, I want you to put that observation into language, into a sentence of sorts. So instead of "red sweater," you might say, "You are wearing a red sweater" or "You've got a red sweater on." How it comes out of your mouth isn't important, so don't try to make a grammatically correct phrase. Simply turn to your partner and describe the first thing you see. It doesn't have to sound good. You might turn to your partner and say, "There's a red sweater, you're wearing it." That's OK.

And what would your partner then repeat? Ah, good question.

Our Palette of Colors: Point of View

As always, you repeat what you hear. But there's a new issue, and it is called *your truthful point of view*. All I want you to know for now is that you must always stick to your own truthful point of view. How does that affect Repetition? Here's an example that illustrates an error that often occurs at this point.

Let's say that you and your partner sit down to work with each other, and you have on a red sweater, and he has on a black shirt. Beginning the repetition exercise, your partner turns to you and says, "You have on a red sweater." Following the guidelines I gave you in chapter 3, you would repeat what you hear, regardless of what you know to be true.

But there's a problem, isn't there? What you both know to be true is that your partner is wearing a black shirt. And since you have already told him that he's wearing a red sweater, it is his job now to hold onto his truthful point of view. He would say, "I don't have on a red sweater." In this way he is still repeating what he heard, but he is changing it enough to make it consistent with his own truthful point of view.

And here's another important ingredient that will help you avoid the error described above. It's called *what's happening*. When your partner started Repetition and said, "You have on a red sweater," who was he talking about in that moment? He was talking about you. That's what was happening; it was about you. So you could repeat what you hear and change it to reflect what was happening in that moment. Thus if he were to say, "You have on a red sweater," what would you say? You would say, "I have on a red sweater." You changed the "you" to "I" because he was talking about you in that moment.

This may sound a little confusing on paper but it will become clearer as you do it together.

Notes on Repetition

Let's review some basic Repetition rules for practice:

1. Let the repetition go back and forth like ping-pong, always repeating what you hear.

2. How do you know when to stop the repetition? Well, when it gets uncomfortable or boring or you just want to stop for any reason, that's a good time to keep going. When you do finally stop, let the other person begin the repetition, and do it some more.

3. The person who begins the repetition must be ruthless with him- or herself about saying the first thing he or she observes. If it's your turn to begin and you feel yourself observing a few things and then choosing one of them to say, stop and start over.

4. Repetition is not about imitating your partner or copying the quality of how he or she sounds. Leave it alone; let the words come out of your mouth.

5. Make sure to take out all pauses as you repeat. Don't rush the exercise, but do repeat what you hear as soon as you actually hear it. This rule will keep you from thinking about the exercise because you will be fully involved in actually doing it.

chapter 5

The Way You See the World

We'll jump into this chapter with a few writing exercises, so please get out your journal. (You don't have to do all three of the exercises today, but I do want you to complete them before reading the rest of this chapter.)

Three Writing Exercises

 Do all the following writing in the form of a free association. What that means is, once you start writing, do not stop. Try to write very quickly and without pausing to figure out what to say. If you don't know what to say, write that. Keep the pen going until you have filled the entire page.

Exercise 1

First, I want you to take your journal to your bedroom. Do that now.

OK, look around your room and find one thing that really makes you feel wonderful when you see it or hold it or think about it.

Have you picked one? Get it and put it in front of you where you are sitting to write. Now take some time to write in your journal about this item and why it makes you so happy. Please do that now and then come back to me.

_____
_____
_____
_____
_____

Exercise 2

For your next assignment, I want you to get today's newspaper or go on the Internet and find an article that makes you so mad you want to scream. When you find one, cut it out or print it out and tape it into your journal. Then I want you to write about the article and in your writing talk about what the article means to you and why it makes you so angry. Please do that now.

_____
_____
_____
_____
_____

Exercise 3

Finally, I want you to write a list of ten things that are extremely important to you. This list can include people in your life, animals, objects, issues—anything you really care about.

After you have the list, I want you to put each one of the things you wrote down on the top of its own page in your journal. When you have done that, I want you to fill each page with your thoughts and feelings about that subject.

When you have completed all ten pages, come back to me and we'll continue with the chapter.

1. _____
2. _____
3. _____
4. _____
5. _____
6. _____
7. _____
8. _____
9. _____
10. _____

Did you enjoy that? Did you discover anything? If you look at all the writing exercises you have just done, what is it that you were exploring? What I had you take a look at was your own point of view.

Point of View, Digging Deeper

What is point of view?

To put it simply, your point of view is the product of all your thoughts, feelings, and attitudes toward the world around you. To continue this investigation, and before we discuss why point of view is such a vital acting component, we are going to move forward in our work on the repetition exercise.

To introduce the next stage of Repetition work, Sanford Meisner told us that "Acting is living truthfully under imaginary circumstances." This is an all-inclusive statement that so clearly defines what the actor's job really is and what it isn't.

> In a time of universal deceit, telling the truth becomes a revolutionary act.
> *George Orwell*

Sandy didn't say, "Give the audience a really slick and clever performance," and he didn't say, "Try to make the audience believe you are the character." He said, first and foremost, the actor's job is to live truthfully.

Live truthfully. Personally, I have always felt that these are the two most profound and beautiful words. And they are certainly the indispensable and fundamental basis of all true acting.

Live truthfully.

These words call on us, challenge us, demand us to bring life to the stage and to do so in a human way. For me, I know that living truthfully is the very core of the fire Meisner ignited in my heart and gut. They are the fuel of these flames that burn as hot and bright as ever.

Now, is living truthfully enough? No, it certainly is not. We must "live truthfully under imaginary circumstances."

To be more specific, is our job as actors about the words? No, acting is not about the words. Acting is about taking on the imaginary circumstances given to us by the playwright, accepting them, and living them out as fully and honestly as we are able. It is about breathing life into the playwright's words, which means taking those words and filling them with behavior—authentic human behavior.

In this chapter, and in all the previous chapters of this book on true acting, we have been wrestling with the "living truthfully" part of "living truthfully under imaginary circumstances." We are spending a lot of time on this because I think it's an important investment.

The Three Moment Game

I am now going to give you a game to play that will serve as a bridge from the repetition you have been doing since our last chapter together to the next stage of Repetition. This exercise is called The Three Moment Game, and it will help us isolate and focus on this thing called behavior. If our job is about human behavior, we better get on very intimate terms with it. Here's how the game works.

You and your partner sit across from each other as you do in Repetition. Pick a person who will begin. The person who will begin (we'll call this person Partner A) thinks up a provocative question to ask the other person, Partner B.

So, the asking of the question is the first moment in The Three Moment Game. Here's an example:

PARTNER A: Are you happy with your life?

Partner B must repeat the question immediately, allowing himself to have whatever response he has to it. It is very important, Partner B, that you repeat the question immediately, without any pause. This takes away any possibility of thinking about how you should respond to the question.

Also, you must never try to have a response to the question; you must simply allow yourself to have whatever response you actually have in that moment. So now our example looks like this:

PARTNER A: Are you happy with your life?
PARTNER B: (*Repeating immediately, his eyebrows rise and his lips get tight.*) Am I happy with my life?

Partner A, your job now is to figure out what Partner B's response to the question was, from your point of view. What I mean is, Partner A, you must state to Partner B what Partner B's behavior meant to you.

At first, talk it out a little bit, out loud and directly to Partner B. Then finish by telling Partner B in a simple and direct way what his behavior "said" to you. Let me take our example and make this very clear. Here's how it might look:

> PARTNER A: Are you happy with your life?
>
> PARTNER B: (*Repeating immediately, his eyebrows rise and his lips get tight.*) Am I happy with my life?
>
> PARTNER A: (*Reflects and, speaking out loud, she figures out the meaning of Partner B's behavior.*) Well, I got that you didn't like being asked that question, uhh, that it really wasn't any of my business. Yeah, that's the strongest thing I got, so I would say: (*She concludes with a direct and simple statement.*) You don't think that's any of my business.

And that's it, three moments: A asks the question, B repeats the question, allowing his response to it, and then A says what B's response meant to her.

Do not then discuss it. Simply move on to another Three Moment Game with the other person taking the first moment.

Notes on The Three Moment Game

As you work on this, there are a few important things I want you to know:

1. Don't rush to the answer that's in the third moment.

To make this point, let me use our example exercise in a new way:

> PARTNER A: Are you happy with your life?
>
> PARTNER B: (*Repeating immediately, his eyes light up and he smiles.*) Am I happy with my life?
>
> PARTNER A: You are happy with your life.

In this example, Partner A saw instantly in Partner B's behavior the answer to his question. That will happen sometimes, but in this game, we are more interested in the behavior that gives you the answer than the answer itself.

So don't rush to the answer. Take the time to try and figure out how your partner's behavior spoke to you, what it meant to you. With that in mind, the example might look like this:

> PARTNER A: Are you happy with your life?
>
> PARTNER B: (*Repeating immediately, his eyes light up and he smiles.*) Am I happy with my life?

> PARTNER A: (*Reflects and, speaking out loud, she figures out the meaning of Partner B's behavior.*) I saw you smile and your eyes brighten like you really were pleased to have a chance to answer the question. You looked delighted. Yeah, yeah, that's it. (*She concludes with a direct and simple statement.*) You are delighted!

2. There is always some response.

Sometimes you may ask the question and not much happens over there with your partner when he repeats the question. In this instance, many students say, "I don't know what that behavior was. I didn't see anything happen."

What I want you to know is that there is never nothing; there is always something.

The response you get from your partner after you ask the provocative question is always exactly what it is. What I mean is, if you ask a question and your partner repeats it with a blank expression and no vocal inflection, your statement to him might be something like, "You are unmoved" or "That bores you" or "That leaves you blank."

You always work with what you get, never more and never less. This is why it is important that Partner A asks provocative questions. Remember, the point is to provoke a response in Partner B. In this way, it is an artificial exercise because you know, if you're Partner B, that you are going to be asked a question and you know that you are supposed to allow your response to it. But isn't that always true in theater? Isn't it always true that the actor already knows?

Yes, it is. The actor knows but must not know. What do I mean?

Well, let's say you are in a play, and there is a scene in which your long-lost sister knocks at your door, and you are supposed to be totally surprised to see her when you open the door. Is it not true that you, the actor, already actually know who is at the door?

Of course you do. You have rehearsed it a zillion times, and you know the moment when the knock is supposed to happen, and you know that it is the actor playing your sister who will be out there knocking. But your job is to live out that moment as if you do not know.

So, the truth is you know and you must not know. That's our job as actors every time we step onto the stage—to live out these events as if it was the first time they have ever occurred. Your audience members are not paying to see last night's' performance!

3. Trust your intuitive perceptions.

If you are the partner asking the question, I want you to know that how your partner's behavior speaks to you isn't limited to something you see in his physical response.

Sometimes you have a feeling in your gut about what the question did to him. You have a sense of what happened over there, but you can't really say you got it from anything that you noticed in him physically. Behavior isn't limited to just the physical, and how you perceive behavior isn't limited to physical signals that you are consciously aware of receiving.

Often, something happens in a person somewhere inside her that is communicated to you in a very clear and powerful way, but not in a way that you could describe. I want you to be aware that this is also happening in our Three Moment Game. The more you work through the process I am sharing with you, the more you will come to trust that intuitive part of yourself.

If you practice it, The Three Moment Game will begin to help you strengthen your own availability to what is happening with your partner in each moment, from your point of view.

> Your vision will become clear only when you look into your heart. Who looks outside, dreams. Who looks inside, awakens.
> *Carl Jung*

That's important. Your description of your partner's response in the third moment of the exercise is always delivered from your point of view. Is it right or wrong? It's not about right or wrong. It's about what is true from your point of view.

You have every right to your own truthful point of view no matter what anybody else says. Now, the other person may disagree with you. That's fine. He may even change your mind, who knows. With The Three Moment Game, we are working on you becoming more present to what's happening with your partner and more expressive, in a simple, clear, and very direct way, of your own truthful point of view.

That's powerful. Not only is it powerful, it is absolutely essential that, as an acting student, you begin to get deeply in touch with your own truthful point of view. Why? Because, as an actor, that's all you have. Unlike the writer, the musician, or the sculptor, you don't have a typewriter in front of you, guitar strings under your fingers, or a chisel in your hand. Your authentic point of view is, in fact, your own unique palette of colors with which you will create.

You may say. "Well, what about my voice and my body, how I sound and move?" And I say to you that everything, all of it, must spring from your own truthful point of view. "But," you say, "I am playing a character."

Look out, there's that dangerous word: character. Many young acting students are taught that to be a character they must give him a limp, or maybe some eccentricity of speech, or possibly some creative makeup. Character has nothing to do with doing a limp. The way a character moves, talks, looks—these things are simply technical demands, like if you had to work on a dialect for a part or play a person who is blind.

Now, if you say to me, "But Larry, doesn't having a limp or a speech problem affect and influence who this character is and how they experience the world they live in?" "Aaaah," I say. "Now you're on to something!"

chapter 6

What They Do Matters

To review a bit, we explored the fact that the basis, the foundation of all great acting is what we call the "reality of doing." That means when you do something as an actor, you really do it. This may seem like a simple statement. I promise you that it's profound.

I have also said to you that as actors, we must be more concerned with the attempt than with the results. That, in fact, the quality of our acting depends on how fully we bring ourselves to the attempt to accomplish something onstage. (Notice that I did not say the quality of our acting depends on how emotional we are. That's an important note, and we'll come back to it later in this chapter.)

The simple fact is that acting is doing, and when we are not actively involved in doing something onstage, we are no longer acting.

What exactly do I mean by *doing*? To answer that, I am going to suggest that you do an investigation of your own behavior and activities. Here are three assignments for you to try before we proceed.

Assignment 1

👁 During the next twenty-four hours, catch yourself—make a detached, objective observation about yourself—as you are doing five physical activities, for example, getting dressed, washing dishes, eating dinner, and so on.

As you are doing each of these things, bring to your awareness how fully you are really involved with whatever you are doing. That is, are you completely engaged with this activity, or is some of your attention on other concerns as well?

When you have made this observation about five different activities, write in your journal about what you have discovered. Then go to the next assignment.

_____
_____
_____
_____
_____
_____
_____
_____
_____

Assignment 2

 During the next few days, I want you to catch yourself in at least five different encounters with people in your life.

We make contact with others in many different ways: you might be in conversation with a friend; you might be sitting silently next to a classmate when the two of you glance toward each other and share a moment; you might be behind a stranger in a line somewhere and the two of you connect in some way.

Notice what you are trying to accomplish in these moments with the other person. You will find that sometimes what you want to have happen will be very clear to you. For example, imagine that you are trying to watch your favorite TV show and your little brother is being a real pain in the neck. So you tell him, with great enthusiasm, "Hey, Mom brought home some of that great vanilla pudding you love. It's in the fridge right now." As he runs off to raid the refrigerator, you might stop to examine what you just did. It would probably be clear to you that you were simply using the pudding to get your brother off your back so you could enjoy your TV show.

Sometimes, though, what you are doing with another person—what you are really doing, under the surface—will be much more subtle. You might be talking with your best friend, who has been spending a lot of time with someone else lately. After you walk away from her, you stop and realize that, although you were only talking about clothes and hair, underneath every one of your words you were actually trying to get her to tell you in some way that she still likes you the best.

For this assignment, take some time to write in your journal after each encounter and explore what you found yourself involved in doing with the other person—what you wanted from that person, what you wanted to have happen, or what you wanted to accomplish. When you have observed five different encounters in that way, come back for the next assignment.

___

Assignment 3

Now, take a look at five more encounters with people; only this time, I want you to take note of what it is they are trying to accomplish with you.

For example, perhaps your mother seems a little distant and cool toward you one afternoon, and you sense that underneath all her questions about your day at school, she is really trying to communicate to you that she expects and is waiting for an apology from you for something that you did the night before.

> Again, after each encounter, write in your journal what you thought the other person was doing, what response he or she wanted from you, or what he or she wanted to have happen.

_____
_____
_____
_____
_____
_____
_____
_____

OK, let's talk about these assignments.

Multitasking Ain't So Hot

The purpose of the first assignment was to begin to give you an experience of how often we are not fully involved in the things we are doing.

You are doing your homework, while you're talking on the phone with a friend, while you're watching television, while you're painting your nails, while you're thinking about how you really don't want to go with your family to visit Uncle Moe on Saturday.

We rarely do one thing fully because we have become accustomed to doing many things partially! It's an unfortunate truth, because it means that we never really have the complete experience of anything in life. How can you possibly enjoy being with your friend on the phone if you are trying to watch television? How can you enjoy the show if you are busy thinking about how you don't want to go to Uncle Moe's on Saturday?

And when you get to Uncle Moe's, how can you enjoy the food that's served for dinner if you're busy thinking about what you're going to wear to the dance next Friday?

What would it be like to really give your full attention to that delicious potato you're eating, as you're eating it? For that matter, what would it be like to really listen and be fully present to Uncle Moe when he tells that well-worn story one more time? Who knows, it could be amazing. It could be amazing because, even if you've heard the story twenty times, chances are you have never really listened to it with your full attention. Try it some time. It is a simple life truth that it is impossible to do two things fully at the same time.

Since the quality of your acting depends on how fully you are doing what you are doing, this is a very important truth for actors to understand.

> If you greatly desire something, have the guts to stake everything on obtaining it.
> Marcus Tullius Cicero

What this means is that when you are doing "this," you must be doing it 100 percent. If something else should demand your attention, you must then do "that" at 100 percent. You must always do whatever it is you are doing at 100 percent until something else has a strong enough pull to take you away from it.

This kind of focus and concentration isn't foreign to human nature. Watch an infant sometime. You'll see that she does everything at 100 percent. When she plays with a rattle, she is doing nothing but playing with a rattle. When she looks at you and laughs, she is doing only that one thing. When she discovers her fingers and studies her thumb, her thumb is the only thing in the world at that moment.

The infant gives everything she does her complete, relaxed, and undivided attention until her attention is pulled to something else.

What Are You Doing Right Now?

I'm hoping that you are beginning to see—when you were doing assignments two and three—that in life, we are always involved in something we are doing, something we are trying to accomplish or trying to make happen. True acting puts that fact under a microscope and requires us to become relentlessly "active" in our acting.

In life, we often forget how much is at stake. As actors, the stakes are always high and what we must accomplish is always urgent. The word *casual* has no part in the world of acting. There is no casual moment onstage. Even if two characters appear to be having a "casual" conversation, believe me, what these two people need to accomplish is vital, essential, and pressing!

Clearly, if you are to do something fully, you must give it your complete attention. Now, when your complete attention is on what you are doing, it cannot be on yourself. But because most actors are more interested in themselves than the other person onstage, they are constantly measuring their own performance and thinking about how wonderful they are and what a dynamic and powerful performance they are giving. What crap! I bring this up now because I see so many actors with their attention on themselves rather than on the thing they are supposed to be doing. What this means is that they're not really doing anything! Of course, this is not acting. It is not even related to acting. It is emotional masturbation, and it's not a pretty sight.

The great gift of really and fully doing something is that your emotions come to life on their own, humanly and organically. I want you to remember that acting is about what you are doing; it is never about what you are feeling.

The Three Moment Game into Repetition: Crossing the Bridge

Let's return to the repetition exercise we have been working on together and move forward in this work. We have worked on The Three Moment Game. To review, briefly:

In the first moment, Partner A asks a provocative question. In the second, Partner B repeats the question, allowing herself to have whatever reaction she has to it. In the third moment, Partner A reflects on Partner B's response and then articulates what it means to him.

Now we will continue the development of the game. We'll do this in a few stages. First, I want you to adjust the third moment.

Instead of taking your time in the third moment to figure out what your partner's behavior meant to you, as we did in the last session, I want you to respond immediately. Here's an example of what this might look like:

> PARTNER A: (*Asking the provocative question.*) Have you ever killed a cat?
> PARTNER B: (*Repeating the question immediately, her eyes open wide.*) Have I ever killed a cat?
> PARTNER A: (*Immediately stating to Partner B what her response meant to him.*) You are shocked.

The important difference is that now, Partner A is not taking any time to consider what Partner B's behavior "said" to him. He must respond immediately, with no pause or reflection at all.

 I want you and your partner to do this eight times, and then come back here for the next stage.

Did you do it eight times? Really? Don't kid me now . . .

 OK, Here's the next step. This time, the third moment will lead into Repetition. Here's what it looks like:

PARTNER A: (*Asking the provocative question.*) Have you ever killed a cat?
PARTNER B: (*Repeating the question immediately, her eyes open wide.*) Have I ever killed a cat?
PARTNER A: (*Immediately stating to Partner B what her response meant to him.*) You are shocked.
  (*And without a pause, the partners go into Repetition.*)
PARTNER B: I am shocked.
PARTNER A: You are shocked
PARTNER B: I am shocked.
PARTNER A: You are shocked
PARTNER B; I am shocked.
PARTNER A: You are shocked.
PARTNER B: I am shocked
PARTNER A: You are shocked.
PARTNER B: I am shocked.
PARTNER A: You are shocked.

Do that level of The Three Moment Game a few times and then continue to the next step.

Now that you have practiced allowing The Three Moment Game to lead you into Repetition, I want you to do the same thing with one important addition.

Working Off Behavior

This time, as you get into Repetition, I want you to know that as you repeat, the repetition can change when it must change.

What do I mean by that? As you are doing Repetition, new things will be happening with your partner, and you must be available to whatever is actually happening over there.

When you become aware of a change in your partner, the repetition must change too. Let me take the example exercise we've been using and show you what this might look like:

> PARTNER A: (*Asking the provocative question.*) Have you ever killed a cat?
> PARTNER B: (*Repeating the question immediately, her eyes open wide.*) Have I ever killed a cat?
> PARTNER A: (*Immediately stating to Partner B what her response meant to him.*) You are shocked.
> (*And without a pause, the partners go into repetition, responding to what is happening with the partner.*)
> PARTNER B: I am shocked
> PARTNER A: You are shocked.
> PARTNER B: I am shocked.
> PARTNER A: You are shocked
> PARTNER B: I am shocked
> PARTNER A: (*He giggles.*) You are shocked.
> PARTNER B: That amuses you.
> PARTNER A: That amuses me.
> PARTNER B: That amuses you.
> PARTNER A: That amuses me.
> PARTNER B: (*Crinkles her eyebrows.*) That amuses you?
> PARTNER A: You don't understand.
> PARTNER B: I don't understand.
> PARTNER A: You don't understand.
> PARTNER B: (*Raising her voice.*) I don't understand.
> PARTNER A: You're offended.
> PARTNER B: I am offended.
> PARTNER A: You really mean that.
> PARTNER B: I really do mean that.

PARTNER A: (*Stares back.*) You do really mean that.
PARTNER B: You are just so puzzled.
PARTNER A: I am just so puzzled.
PARTNER B: That makes you mad.
PARTNER A: That makes me mad.
PARTNER B: That makes you mad
PARTNER A: That makes me mad
PARTNER B: That makes you mad.

> Notice that the repetition doesn't change because you want it to. It changes when it must change. And why does the repetition change? Because of something you get back from your partner. Practice this version of the game for a while and then come back to me.

Now that you have had this experience, you will simply do Repetition no longer using The Three Moment Game. The Three Moment Game was a bridge that took us from the repetition we were doing before to the repetition we have arrived at today.

So how do you do Repetition now, without The Three Moment Game? It's simple: You both sit down and you begin.

Who starts? Whoever starts will start.

How do you begin? You both take what you get from your partner, and someone will begin. Then off you go together on the roller-coaster ride of Repetition.

It Takes Practice, Relentless Practice

The more you do Repetition, the more available you will become to what is happening with your partner in each moment and the more immediately you will be able to respond. This is called *working off your partner*.

The important thing right now is that you must not try to find the things to work off of. You must simply work off what you get when you are aware of it. This is very important, because if you are busy trying to find things to work off of, you will be missing all the things that are really happening over there. Trying to find something to respond to requires an expenditure of effort, and Repetition is really effortless.

Why? Repetition actually needs no effort because your partner will dish up everything you need. You just have to be there to receive it. I did not say that this is easy; it's not. But acting must become effortless, like all great art. That's why you must practice your exercises rigorously and go beyond what is reasonable. When it is most difficult to get yourself to practice, that's when you need to practice most of all. Only through unceasing hard work can you arrive at the place of true effortlessness.

And that's where the joy is! The Joy!

> All joy emphasises our pilgrim status; always reminds, beckons, awakens desire. Our best havings are wantings.
> C. S. Lewis

chapter 7

Is Anything Behind Those Words?

The playwright gives you the words. Now, how do you bring them to life?

Acting is an intensely personal endeavor. Our thoughts, our emotions and spirit, and our physical selves make the music. Unfortunately, many actors are never trained to work intimately and personally. Many students are pushed toward unhealthy, artificial, and inhuman ways of working because many acting teachers (and directors) do not understand what it is that really communicates from the stage.

When I say "really communicates," I am talking about reaching the audience where they live: in their minds, hearts, and guts. I am talking about offering the audience an experience that shifts something inside them so that when they leave the theater, they are not the same people they were when they arrived.

As a theater artist, this is always my goal. I am always striving to create a work that is vitally alive, human, and rich.

Well, the truth is, not every teacher or director and not every actor is interested in working this way. Why? Because there is a price to pay: The cost is personal and the cost is high. Very high. Not everyone is willing to invest himself in this way. Not everyone is willing to pay the price.

Ultimately, you don't choose to work this way; it chooses you. You will find that if you turn out to be one of those rare actors who ceaselessly pursue this thing we have labeled "true acting," you do so not because you want to but because you have to.

From You to the Audience

So what is it, do you think, that really communicates from the stage?

Yes, the audience is certainly affected by the physical production of the play, such as costumes, sets, and lighting. They are also affected by the physical presence of the actors, including their bodies, movement, and voices. The audience receives the play's literal story as told to them by the actors speaking words the playwright has provided.

> Truth is heavy,
> so few men carry it.
> *folk saying*

What I want to impress upon you is that all these things—all of them—are empty and hollow without the crucial acting ingredient that we are here to investigate today. And what is that?

Let me begin to answer with a statement I made before:

Acting is not about the words.

It is important that I tell you this again because many actors have mistaken notions about what their job is. The words are the job of the playwright. The actor's job is to bring these words to life through the vehicle of authentic human behavior, so if behavior is the key, where does our behavior spring from?

I want to share something with you. It's from a great book called *The Empty Space* by Peter Brook, and this particular paragraph is very important. Brook says:

> A word does not start as a word—it is an end product which begins as an impulse, stimulated by attitude and behavior which dictate the need for expression. This process occurs inside the dramatist; it is then repeated inside the actor. Both may only be conscious of the words, but both for the author and then for the actor the word is a small visible portion of a gigantic unseen formation. Some writers attempt to nail down their meaning and intentions in stage directions and explanations, yet we cannot help being struck by the fact that the best dramatists explain themselves the least. They recognize that the only way to find the true path to the speaking of a word is through a process that parallels the original creative one. This can neither be bypassed nor simplified.

That is a profound statement. (If you are an acting teacher, it's a great place to kick off some class discussion.)

Please take out your acting journal, read the Brook quote a few more times, and write down some of your responses.

_____
_____
_____
_____
_____

True Acting Is More about the Unseen Than the Seen

What Brook is really telling us actors is that the words are the least of our problems. In fact, the words are merely the tip of the iceberg, they are just a "small visible portion of a gigantic unseen formation." I love that. For me, "a gigantic unseen formation" underscores the fact that, in the end, the nature of true creation onstage is secret and mysterious.

Importantly, Peter Brook reminds us of the truth that words appear and are necessary only after a significant chain of events.

What are those occurrences? Brook says that words are "the end product which begins as an impulse, stimulated by attitude and behavior which dictate the need for expression." If you take a look back at the earlier chapters in this book, you will notice that this is exactly the progression of acting skills we have been exploring together.

1. We started by looking at **impulse** or a return to your uninhibited, uncensored, and spontaneous self.
2. Then we moved on to **attitude**, which is your absolutely individual and unique point of view toward the world around you and which is the key component of how you respond to everything you encounter.
3. After that, we dove into the realm of **behavior**, which is a result of everything you actually think and feel and what you are specifically trying to accomplish in each moment.

The combination of these three elements, as Brook writes, "dictates the need for expression."

Isn't that great? The need for expression! Suddenly you see that acting is not about simply learning your lines and saying them in some way that seems to sound sensible. You must, in fact, have an authentic need to say those words. Listen carefully. You must have the authentic *need* to speak the words!

And I'll tell you, very few actors do. Very, very few.

Living, Breathing and Taking Action

Well, we've got a challenge on our hands, friends, but it's a great one. Let me be blunt about this. Certainly "trying to accomplish" something creates a need for expression. In acting terms, you might call this your *action* or *objective*, an essential acting element no matter what you call it.

> Someone to tell it to is one of the fundamental needs of human beings.
> Miles Franklin

The problem is that acting students everywhere are taught the "what" of an action: "Play your action. Play your action. What is your action?" This is a very big mistake. Anybody can play an action. But few acting students are taught ways to investigate the "why." Why do you need to do that, and why do you need to do that right now?

And I am not talking about you the "character." I am speaking to you the actor who had to go to the bathroom three times before walking out onto the stage, you the actor who put so much effort into getting your hair just right before leaving the wings, you the actor who screamed for joy and called home to tell your parents when you found out that you were cast in the play.

Why do you, the human being who is also an actor, have the hunger and the need to do this specific thing you are doing right now?

Huge numbers of recent college and university acting program graduates who have auditioned for me over the years know how to "play in action." There is a clear consistency to their audition pieces. The monologues are like a beaded string of superficially chosen objectives performed through sounds and movements intellectually devised with the hopes that the performance will be "interesting." Sometimes, these pretenders are quite slick.

These young actors are perhaps the saddest to me because they actually believe they are really doing something.

These kinds of audition performances are never interesting; they are distressing. Since nothing on the stage is holding my attention, my mind wanders, and I notice that old chair over there that was used in a production five years ago, and I wish that I had remembered to take it to the dump last week. But wait.

What You Know and What You Don't Know: Both Are Revealed

Suddenly, in walks a young actor who stands on the stage and barely moves. Before a word is spoken, I know something very different is happening in the room. This person speaks quietly and simply, yet I am riveted to her and deeply moved by how desperately important what she is saying is to her, by how strong her actual need is to say those words and fulfill her deeper wish.

And the difference between the slick pretender and the authentic actor is, to borrow a metaphor from David Mamet, like the difference between looking at a fluorescent lightbulb and gazing into a wood-burning fire.

What creates this difference? The only thing that meaningfully communicates from the stage is "what you really know." In other words, the actor must really know what he's talking about or else it's a big lie. And, believe me, no matter how slick you are, the audience knows deep down that they are being lied to. Sanford Meisner said, "It's never about showing, it's always about knowing."

 What exactly does it mean to say that you must "really know" what you are talking about when you work on stage? Let's explore this with some writing exercises. I want you to get your journal and put each of the following statements on the top of its own page:

Page 1. I once was happier than I have ever been. This is what happened . . .

Page 2. A time I was really angry with my parents was when they . . .

Page 3. One time, I cried and cried because . . .

Page 4. The most fun I ever had was when I . . .

Now that you have four new pages in your journal, I want you to write, in as much detail as possible, about each of these statements. Take all the time you need, and if you run out of room on one page, continue on another. After you have completed all four writing assignments, resume our chapter together.

1. I once was happier than I have ever been. This is what happened . . .

_____
_____
_____
_____
_____
_____
_____
_____
_____
_____

2. A time I was really angry with my parents was when they . . .

_____
_____
_____
_____
_____
_____
_____
_____
_____

3. One time, I cried and cried because . . .

_____
_____
_____
_____
_____
_____
_____
_____

4. The most fun I ever had was when I . . .

_____
_____
_____
_____
_____
_____
_____
_____
_____

To be very simple, where would we say your responses to the four writing assignments came from? I say your responses came from "what you really know."

That's obvious, right? As you moved your pen across the paper, you didn't have to work real hard to invent anything because the things you wrote about actually live in you. And, as you turned your attention to that place in yourself where these particular things live, the words came to you in a most natural way.

> You can kiss your family and friends good-bye and put miles between you, but at the same time you carry them with you in your heart, your mind, your stomach, because you do not just live in a world but a world lives in you.
> *Frederick Buechner*

Suppose you were here in front of me, and we were having a conversation. If I asked you to tell me all about your grandmother, everything you tell me would come from what you actually know to be true. Even if you were to say, "Well, I never really knew my grandmother. She died when I was only a few months old," that too would come from what you really know. And as I listen to you speak, I would notice all kinds of things about the meaning of your grandmother to you and your relationship with her. These things would be communicated to me without you consciously trying to convey them in any way.

Why? Because you are simply speaking from what you really know.

The Gifts of Horton Foote

Listen to the following words from the beautiful play *A Young Lady of Property*, written by my dear friend and favorite playwright, the late Horton Foote who during his life gave all of us the great gift of his heart and his humanity through his beautiful plays. It would be a great idea for you to get the play and read it!

The following lines are from a scene between best friends Wilma and Arabella, two teenage girls who have been accepted to go to Los Angeles for a Hollywood screen test. Arabella doesn't really want to leave but has gone along with Wilma's plan because she is desperately afraid she will lose Wilma's friendship if she says no.

This scene takes place on the swing in front of the house Wilma lived in when her mother was alive.

> ARABELLA: Oh, I almost forgot. Your Aunt Gert said for you to come on home.
> WILMA: I'll go in a little. I love to swing in my front yard. Aunt Gert has a swing in her front yard, but it's not the same. Mama and I used to come out here and swing together. Some nights when Daddy was out all night gambling, I used to wake up and hear her out here swinging away. Sometimes she'd let

> me come and sit beside her. We'd swing until three or four in the morning. The pear tree looks sickly, doesn't it? The fig trees are doing nicely though. I was out in the back and the weeds are near knee high, but the fig trees just seem to thrive in the weeds. The freeze must have killed off the banana trees. Maybe I won't leave either. Maybe I won't go to Hollywood after all.
>
> ARABELLA: You won't?
>
> WILMA: No, Maybe I shouldn't. That just comes to me now. You know sometimes my old house looks so lonesome it tears at my heart. I used to think it looks lonesome just whenever it had no tenants, but now it comes to me it has looked lonesome ever since Mama died and we moved away, and it will look lonesome until some of us move back here. Of course, Mama can't, and Daddy won't. So it's up to me.

When Wilma talks to Arabella about how she used to swing with her mother, she speaks from what she really knows. And I'll tell you, the actress playing Wilma has to earn the right to say a line as rich and potent as "sometimes my old house looks so lonesome it tears at my heart."

This brings us to the key question. Wilma has had her own unique experiences, thoughts, and feelings. But if you are the actress playing Wilma, you don't have those exact experiences, thoughts, and feelings. So, although Wilma knows what she is talking about when she speaks those words, how do you, the actor, arrive at a place where you too know what you are talking about when you speak the words that Foote has provided for you?

A great question, isn't it? And that's the topic for the following chapter!

chapter 8

Do You Know What You Are Talking About?

We have been talking about the acting challenge of getting inside the words you speak onstage and knowing what you are talking about. Again, when I say *knowing*, I am not talking about anything related to knowing your lines or knowing facts like one plus one equals two.

And, by the way, if you are looking for a way to squeeze acting into a one-plus-one-equals-two kind of formula, I suggest you give that one up right away. There are no easy answers or paint-by-number methods that work for everyone all the time. You must eventually build your own very personal craft of acting as you take "this" from over here and "that" from over there and a little something from somewhere else, until you have discovered a way of working that fits with your own inner makeup.

Exploring Character

It is time now for us to begin to deal with the text of the play and to begin to work on understanding the character from the play.

What is a character? A character is a human being with a particular point of view and a unique and deep need to fulfill something. The character lives in the specific set of imaginary circumstances given to us by the playwright.

This is a good time to alert you to the dangers of an acting exercise that is given to many high school and college acting students. It is the famous "write the biography of your character" exercise—you know, where you invent the character's blood type, describe the wallpaper they had when they were five, "remember" when they learned to tie their shoelaces, and so on and so on. Have you done that one?

As a way of creating a character, the intellectual "character biography" is not only a waste of your time, but also potentially harmful because you are often doing nothing more than filling up your head with useless information. As one of my great acting teachers used to say, "How's that gonna help you get out of the dressing room?"

So then, how do you begin to really make a personal connection with the character you are going to play? How do you find your way in?

The thing I want you to know is that you will never really "be" the character. Nor is acting "believing." What is it then? Acting is actually a process of accepting the imaginary circumstances and living them out as if they were true. (There's the big "as if" we inherited from Stanislavsky.)

The distinction between believing and accepting is an important one. Believing is something that happens in your head, a conscious intellectual process. Accepting happens in what I will call your creative center; it is a process that goes much deeper than conscious thought. The key is to learn how to nourish that creative place in yourself in ways that bring you more closely in line with the particular point of view of the character.

A specific point of view is the essence of character. Of course, sometimes the point of view of the character may be very similar to your own, and sometimes it will be very, very different.

How the Character Sees the World

To help you begin to get on intimate terms with the character's point of view and to start the process of knowing what you are talking about onstage, I want to give you two simple exercises that I have found to be very useful. To do this, I will use the text I shared with you in the previous chapter from the Horton Foote play *A Young Lady of Property*. Here again are the lines from the play.

> ARABELLA: Oh, I almost forgot. Your Aunt Gert said for you to come to come on home.
> WILMA: I'll go in a little. I love to swing in my front yard. Aunt Gert has a swing in her front yard, but it's not the same. Mama and I used to come out here

and swing together. Some nights when Daddy was out all night gambling, I used to wake up and hear her out here swinging away. Sometimes she'd let me come and sit beside her. We'd swing until three or four in the morning. The pear tree look sickly, doesn't it? The fig trees are doing nicely though. I was out in the back and the weeds are near knee high, but fig trees just seem to thrive in the weeds. The freeze must have killed off the banana trees. Maybe I won't leave either. Maybe I won't go to Hollywood after all.

ARABELLA: You won't?

WILMA: No. Maybe I shouldn't. That just comes to me now. You know sometimes my old house looks so lonesome it tears at my heart. I used to think it looks lonesome just whenever it had no tenants, but now it comes to me it has looked lonesome ever since Mama died and we moved away, and it will look lonesome until some of us move back here. Of course, Mama can't, and Daddy won't. So it's up to me.

Exercise 1: The Key Phrases

Please get a copy of *A Young Lady of Property*. You are playing Wilma. (If you are a guy, you can still work on this part as a way to learn these techniques.) The first exercise I want to give you is The Key Phrases. Here's how it works.

> Go through the play and write down a list of all the things your character says that you feel are vital to understanding what is most meaningful to the person. As you do this, write down the exact words that the character speaks; do not paraphrase.

_____

_____

_____

_____

_____

_____

Sometimes something that another character says can be a key phrase for your character. Most of the time, though, the key phrases will be things your character says. If you do use something that another character says, be sure it clarifies your character's point of view and not that of the character who is speaking it.

Once you have your list, choose three phrases that you feel are the most important and write each of them on its own page.

1. _____
2. _____
3. _____

To show you how this exercise works, I am going to give you a key phrase from one of Wilma's speeches in the section of *A Young Lady of Property* I just shared with you.

Now, before you continue, I want you to be in a place where you can be alone and uninterrupted by anyone and where you can lie down and relax. When you are in that kind of a place, you may continue. (Again, although Wilma is a young woman, for our purposes today, you guys can do this exercise with Wilma's key phrase as well.) Here's the phrase:

"My old house looks so lonesome it tears at my heart."

First, write the phrase down in your book. Then, get in a relaxed position and take another look at the phrase you just wrote down. Now, I am going to ask you to close your eyes and say that phrase to yourself (not out loud) very simply for a few minutes. Do that now, and I will do it along with you.

Did you do that? Did it do something to you?

I believe that phrase is a very potent and powerful line. When I closed my eyes and repeated the phrase to myself, I was moved and shaken inside. All kinds of very personal feelings and images came up: feelings about being a child in the house I grew up in, a deep sadness for a life with my family that no longer exists, and missing a closeness I had that is now at a great distance both physically and emotionally.

✒️ Now, I want you to do the same thing, but this time when you open your eyes, write whatever comes to mind in your journal under the key phrase you were just thinking about.

_____
_____
_____
_____
_____
_____
_____

And that's it. There's no trick here. If you take the key phrases and spend a little time with them each day in the way we have just done, thinking about them with your eyes closed and then writing your response to them, you will begin to personalize the point of view of the character. Again, we are talking about nourishing your own creative center and inviting it to accept and embrace the imaginary circumstances of the play. This is your job as an actor.

Exercise 2: The Key Facts

The next exercise, The Key Facts, builds on the first. While in the first, we were working on personalizing the point of view of the character, now we will be working on developing a personal understanding of the text. And with what aim? It is with the aim of knowing what you are talking about.

Go through the entire play and write down any fact that your character talks about that seems meaningful to the character.

Put each key fact at the top of its own page. Then under the key fact, write down anything your character says about that fact in the rest of the play. Again, use the exact words of the character. As with the key phrases, you won't write down every fact in the play; only those that are meaningful to the character.

For instance, Wilma says that the "fig trees just seem to thrive in the weeds." Well, I would not consider the "weeds" a key fact for Wilma. But let's take the key fact "the swing." Clearly, Wilma has a very strong and personal relationship with the swing! This means that we also will need to have that kind of personal relationship with the swing if we are going to earn the right to speak those words. And here's how to go about it:

I want you to write the key fact "the swing" at the top of a page in your journal. Under it we are going to write what Wilma says about the swing in the lines from the scene above. Do that now.

_____

_____

_____

_____

_____

_____

_____

_____

Got it done? OK, you should now have "the swing" at the top of your page and under it should be:

"I love to swing in my front yard."

"Aunt Gert has a swing in her front yard, but it's not the same."

"Mama and I used to come out here and swing together."

"Some nights when Daddy was out all night gambling. I used to wake up and hear her out here swinging away. Sometimes she'd let me come and sit beside her. We'd swing until three or four in the morning."

Now that you have that, I want you to re-read everything you wrote down, and then underneath it all, I want you to write a free association that is kicked off by all the things Wilma has said about the swing. Write in first person; that is, use "I" instead of "Wilma."

By free association, I mean that you must write whatever comes to you while you are under the influence of what you have just written and read from the point of view of Wilma. This may be a little confusing, but go ahead and give it a try, and I will do the same. Write a short paragraph and come back here, and I will share my free association with you so that you see what it looks like.

_____
_____
_____
_____
_____
_____
_____
_____

Did you do that? Here's what I just wrote:

the swing at night is the safest place to be mommy's arm around me and she whispers in my ear it will all work out all right you don't have to be scared of your father he doesn't realize how he hurts you but he means well and he does care for you but he doesn't know how to show it. You are my love and she kisses my cheek and pulls me tighter to her and the stars are shining I never saw them so bright.

So what's the point? The point is now when I have to talk about the swing, I have a relationship with the swing that is all my own! And what I now know about the swing also lives in the context of the facts of Wilma's life in the play. What I just wrote and discovered about the swing was created by me, and it comes from me!

Do you see? Now when I say the word *swing*, I am talking about that place where I felt safe, where Mommy held me tight and kissed my cheek, where I saw the stars shine so brightly. You see, even with this very preliminary exercise, I now have a personal connection to the swing. I don't ever have to think about what I wrote again or try to do anything about those things I wrote. Because some place inside me created the things I wrote about, those things now live in me.

If I do this every day, take out my journal and write just a little bit more in this way about each of my character's key facts, gradually I will develop a wonderful and personal relationship with the things I speak about in the play, and I will grow closer and closer with the point of view of the character.

Hard Work, Big Rewards

If you do these exercises on a consistent basis, and if you do them in an open way, not trying to shape or control the way your responses come, you will be amazed at the discoveries you will be led to about the play and about your character. You see, there is a part of you that knows more about the character than you could ever think up in your head.

After all of this work is done and you are acting onstage, you don't need to do anything about the personalization work you did at home in your journal; you simply know it. When you really know what you are talking about, the words will resonate in a meaningful way. As one of my students in Brazil said last week in our class, when a person talks from a place of knowing, there is a "density" to their words. I love that and it is very true. There is density!

Knowing what you are talking about will also produce behavior that will be out of your control and uncalculating.

If you are onstage trying to remember the meaning of this or that, or in any way trying to show the audience how much this or that means to you, you are in your head with your attention on yourself. When that happens, you are no longer acting. This is the trap many actors fall into! They are taking their rehearsal process into their performances. But the audience is not paying all that money for tickets to see you do your homework. The audience is paying to see you live fully in the present.

And the great thing about living fully in the present is that you will continually, every night, discover new aspects of your character and his or her relationship to the world of the play. I know, for myself, at the end of a run of a play in which I am acting, I always feel like, "Wait a minute; I don't want to stop now. I'm finally really getting to know this guy!"

The other great thing about living in the present is that the present is where the joy is And, I'll tell you, if you're not having fun onstage, nobody watching you will either! No matter how demanding the role and how painful the circumstances are for the character, the journey you take onstage must be fun for you.

On Talent

There is one more thing to mention here. It has to do with the word *talent*, which I know is of great concern to you.

> Difficult times have helped me to understand better than before, how infinitely rich and beautiful life is in every way, and that so many things that one goes worrying about are of no importance whatsoever . . .
> *Isak Dinesen*

The most important thing you can do to help yourself become the best actor you can possibly be is to work very, very hard. This alone will raise you to the top 5 percent of the acting pool. Talent is a most mysterious thing, and it is something you can do nothing about. What you can do is work your behind off. Working hard will nurture whatever sort of talent you do have.

In the course of your studies and your work, you may come across some very unhappy people. These people will make use of whatever it is they themselves lack and purposely try to make you feel very bad about yourself. If this should happen, get away from these sorts of people as quickly as possible.

Find people to work with who have paid the price themselves, both in their craft and in their personal development. Find teachers who challenge you in a rigorous way, who inspire you and let you know that you are important and that you have a valuable contribution to make on this planet.

The good news is that there are many of these kinds of teachers available to you; teachers who will foster your growth in a direct, honest, and loving way.

chapter 9

The Future of Actor Training

You are the future of acting in this country. So are your teachers. I have written this chapter for your teachers to reflect on the trends of acting and training and some key things to take note of. This conversation is also for you, and I believe it is most useful for you to be aware of the issues your acting teachers may be wrestling with.

The question is "Where is the training of actors headed?," and it is a great one.

I don't know that there is one answer, but I certainly have compelling indications from the teaching trips I have been making to Europe, South America, Canada, and throughout the United States. As I mentioned in the introduction to this book, I have had the great fortune to work with professional actors, professors and heads of university theater departments, directors of professional acting institutes, high school drama teachers, theater and film directors, and screenwriters as well as acting students in both colleges and high schools. One thing I am certain of after all these classes, workshops, and symposiums is that there is a singular, very clear, and powerful desire that connects all of us.

I do believe that this desire is the key to the question I am here to explore with you.

> What makes the engine go? Desire, desire, desire.
> *Stanley Kunitz*

True Acting Defined

Because there are many different opinions about what acting itself should be and which acting techniques are most effective, as promised in chapter 1, I will now describe more specifically what I call True Acting, which, to me, is the essence of all great acting and the aim of all valid acting techniques. And, if we're going to act, striving to be a true actor is the only thing that makes taking the intensely demanding journey worth it.

Intrinsically, the struggle toward true acting will include great depths of suffering. But those who stick with it will discover that on the other side of the pain is boundless joy. If one's desire is to create works of art with lasting value, true acting is the sole path.

> One must not lose desires. They are mighty stimulants to creativeness, to love, and to long life.
> Alexander A. Bogomoletz

As theater educators, it is very important to note that not every student is interested in this pursuit. The student must have an intense interest, must find the work appetizing, and must be willing to purposely venture where it is least comfortable. And without these keen desires, no person on this earth will be willing to pay the price that must be paid. As I have said before, the cost is high. And the cost is personal.

So what is a true actor? A true actor is, first of all, deeply available to his or her partners and to the world around: sensitive, empathic, interested, curious, caring, and continually open. This kind of availability has nothing to do with listening as a technical device; it is what I describe as "listening with the ear of one's heart," which suggests a deeper awareness of what is actually happening with another human being.

Next, just as the playwright infused the blank page with his or her own needs and desires to write the words, the true actor has also worked rigorously, earning the right to speak the words onstage. The actor must find a personal path toward his or her own authentic and human need to say the lines, to listen, and to take action.

Finally, the true actor has also made habitual the ability to fully and honestly inhabit each moment in that moment. And this is no small thing! The life of true acting depends on the actor's ability to be fully available and responsive to what is actually happening, as it is happening. It is urgent and necessary—after all the blocking has been set, after all the lines have been learned, and after all the choices have been personalized and integrated into the performance—that the actor once again enter the unknown so that each night the performance is not an imitative act but a creative one.

Without this, my dear colleagues, the play can be nothing more than a hollow shell: empty, lifeless, corrupt.

Teachers Who Pay the Price

If we are to help guide young actors toward the values of true acting, the teacher and his or her methods of teaching cannot hide behind any intellectual theory or formula. True actor training must be as much a living, breathing entity as acting itself.

To teach from this place, there is a tremendous personal investment required of the teacher and there is no way around it. As a student of Sanford Meisner, I had the experience of being with a teacher who was, in every moment, as personally involved with me in my exercise or scene as was my acting partner. As an actor, I have also worked with some great directors, and they were the same. Peter Brook spoke to this when he said that "[a] real director is someone who climbs down into the pit with the actors and somehow, *together*, they claw their way out."

> Life ought to be a struggle of desire toward adventures whose nobility will fertilize the soul.
> Rebecca West

To me, this kind of personal involvement, which has nothing to do with the intellect or with technique, is what makes teaching acting thrilling and new every time we enter the studio, and it is the primary thing that will assist the acting student in entering uncharted territory and achieving profound growth as an artist.

Also, to teach true acting, the teacher must be a living, breathing example of the very things he or she is attempting to teach to the student. The relationship between the acting teacher and the student must be one of collaboration, where the teacher is continually discovering, moment by moment by moment, what the unique needs of each student are. This demands that the teacher be fully present, available, and deeply caring.

Just as there is a price to pay in becoming a true actor, there is a cost to being the kind of teacher who is able to put his or her ego aside and lead with the deeply held belief that it is more important to help the student become fully who he or she is rather than manipulating a student into becoming like the teacher.

Training as an Invitation

All these things I have described may not be the sole answer to our question "Where is the training of actors headed?," but I am absolutely clear that I have spoken to a deep aching in actors and acting teachers in every part of the world.

Much of the acting and the teaching community has become deeply weary of arguments over technique and frustrated by the cold and lifeless results of various teaching methods in the classroom. On the flip side of the coin, I have also witnessed the great enjoyment some theater instructors get out of arguing about technique and attempting to convince others that their particular system is the best. I have always found these arguments fruitless and boring. Also, it is interesting that many of the most severe attacks come from people who have never actually practiced or personally explored the techniques they are condemning!

> *Those who restrain desire, do so because theirs is weak enough to be restrained.*
> —William Blake

Here is a quote from Herbert Spencer that speaks eloquently about this: "There is a principle which is a bar against all information, which is proof against all arguments and which cannot fail to keep a man in everlasting ignorance. That principle is contempt prior to investigation."

I have experienced this kind of teacher as a person who comes from the attitude that if his neighbor breaks his leg, it will make him, the teacher, walk better. I find this incredibly sad, and of course, this way of approaching life goes against everything our art is about.

As a teacher, I am not here to convince anyone of anything. I think of my work with students, always, as an invitation. The truth about technique, to me, is that if it helps you, great, and if it doesn't, throw it away. Of course, I do have a particular passion for training actors, and my whole adult life has been a devotion to the Meisner Approach, but it is a leaning that comes not from any concept but from my direct experience of a particular path that I was rigorously trained in, which saved my life as an actor and as a human being and which made absolute sense to my insides.

For me, just as I have to earn the right to speak the playwright's words, I believe I can only make a difference in the lives of my students and help them to grow when I teach from a place of true knowing; knowing not as an intellectual theory but as a living, breathing part of my being.

The Inspiration of Gandhi

Here is a story for students and teachers:

> *For many hours, a woman and her eight-year-old son were waiting on a long line to talk with Gandhi. Finally, it was her turn to approach Gandhi and ask*

her question, "Gandhi, my son is causing great trouble in school, and they are threatening to throw him out. The doctor told me that his bad behavior is caused by eating too much sugar." Gandhi looked at the boy and then told the mother, "Bring the boy back to me in two weeks."

Two weeks later, the woman and her son found themselves on another very long line. After many hours, she approached Gandhi once again, "Gandhi, two weeks ago, I told you that my son was going to be thrown out of school if he did not behave and that his behavior was caused by him eating too much sugar." Gandhi looked down at the boy and said, "Stop eating sugar."

As the woman and the boy began to walk away, the mother stopped and turned back to Gandhi, "Gandhi, why did you make us come back today and wait for many hours to speak with you? Why didn't you tell my son to stop eating sugar two weeks ago?" Gandhi replied, "Because until two weeks ago, I too was eating sugar."

On the Meisner Approach

Certainly, grappling with our question on the future of training for actors would be incomplete without my sharing, more specifically, some of my experience with the Meisner work. There are a few main things that would be useful to talk about.

First, we have worked on some of the repetition exercises here in the book, but what is Repetition actually?

> Let us be grateful to people who make us happy, they are the charming gardeners who make our souls blossom.
> *Marcel Proust*

Over the years, I found that many people are not really clear on the ultimate purpose of Repetition. One thing for sure, Repetition is not about "reading behavior." I have often heard this phrase used, and it is misleading because it suggests that Repetition is something technical, like getting good at "reading" the instructions to build an Ikea book shelf. This is not repetition.

I remember, when I was a very young acting student, seeing the great Norwegian actress Liv Ullmann in an interview with Dick Cavett. He asked her how she makes "being in love" in front of a camera so real when it is called for in a scene with another actor. She told him that it simply has to do with "opening herself" to the other actor.

Cavett asked her if she could show him what she was talking about, and she agreed. Then, with out a word, she did exactly what she said. She opened herself to him. In that moment,

I experienced her as being deeply in love with Dick Cavett, and I suddenly found myself sitting on my couch weeping. It was so beautiful, both the overwhelming power of her love and the mastery of this art I was striving to learn.

What I want you to know is that, in those moments of deep connection, when not a word was spoken, Liv Ullmann was, in fact, doing Repetition!

The practice of Repetition must lead toward the ability to be in communion with another human being. It is a sharing at the most intimate, human level. Although the process begins with words, Repetition has nothing to do with speaking at all. Repetition is continually aimed at reawakening the natural and organic human ability for people to be involved with each other, for it is this involvement that then makes words, silence, and all of human behavior necessary.

Like all art, Repetition and the Meisner Approach in all its meticulous step-by-step components are lifting the actor to a spiritual experience where the actor becomes an empty vessel through which something greater than the actor himself can express itself. Through the work, the actor's attention becomes directed completely outward and connected to the world around him, with no need to control or manipulate anyone as he fights with his life to achieve the mission he has set out on, the mission that was inspired by the script and has now become truly his own.

The Human Touch

As I discussed earlier in this book, it is my own belief that if you want to be a better actor, first be a better person.

> Basically, the only thing we need is a hand that rests on our own, that wishes it well, that sometimes guides us.
> *Hector Bianciotti*

As I have been teaching around this country, and other countries, this is a value that has become a primary concern for actors and teachers. I am thrilled with the movement in this direction because the act of creating theater must be rooted first in human values or it is false.

It is not that theater is an imitation of our lives; it's not. Theater, as Sandy told us, demands a greater truth. What is this greater truth? It is a basic life truth; the things that we know in our hearts have lasting value, always come to us—not on our own or by ourselves but as a gift through our connection with someone else. The best things in life, in my point of view (and certainly this has been my experience time and time again), are surprising, unexpected, and greater than we could have imagined—and they are always the result of being in relationship with others.

When we seriously consider the path toward true satisfaction and fulfillment in this life, we can see that this path always travels through someone else. It is the same with acting. Acting does not fuel our acting, and it never has. Without our humanity as the key, the impulse to act will fade because it is shallow and limited, and it's just not much fun. And if it's not fun, why bother?

The other part of this "greater truth" has to do with some essential things most people have forgotten—having gone to sleep or, as in *The Matrix*, having become batteries in the machine. Great theater and true acting can unplug the audience from the machine for a moment in time. In this moment, the audience is served a wake-up call to the simple truth that the stakes are high; that every choice matters; that we cannot afford to live life as an assumption; that we do care very much; that our capacity to love each other is vast; that we are under the pressure of the darkness all around us; that the closer we get to fulfilling our true desires, the pressure from the darkness gets more intense; that in the face of this fierce opposition we have the strength to do what is moral and right; that we can go on; and that we are not alone.

> The size of your success is measured by the strength of your desire; the size of your dream; and how you handle disappointment along the way.
> *Robert Toru Kiyosaki*

Sense of Purpose

Please remember that all jobs have one thing in common: They were brought into existence because they are supposed to make a difference in someone else's life.

Acting is a job. When an actor has bolstered herself to work in the space I call true acting, she actually does make a difference in the lives of the people who witness her. As David Mamet said, "People come to the theater to be reminded that authentic communication between two human beings is still possible!" Our students need to be reminded. They need to know that when they work simply and honestly and with meaning, they are not just making a wonderful production for people to come experience and enjoy, but that they themselves are *the gift*.

And lastly, as an eloquent saying goes, "Education is not the filling of a pail, but the lighting of a fire."

> Education is not the filling of a pail, but the lighting of a fire.
> William Butler Yeats

Let's always strive, you and I, to teach from this place. Let's always remember that respect and compassion are fundamental, and that our students will grow in their courage to fulfill their gifts to the extent that we work with them from a place of love and admiration. Let's always make clear the requirement for hard work in our classrooms and never be willing to accept less.

Thank you all for your attention and healthy travels on your journey.

chapter 10

More Quotes to Challenge and Inspire

Dwell not upon thy weariness, thy strength shall be according to the measure of thy desire.

proverb

It is the nature of desire not to be satisfied, and most men live only for the gratification of it.

Aristotle

Man is the only animal whose desires increase as they are fed; the only animal that is never satisfied.

Henry George

One must desire something to be alive.

Margaret Deland

Desire creates the power.

Raymond Holliwell

If men could regard the events of their own lives with more open minds, they would frequently discover that they did not really desire the things they failed to obtain.

André Maurois

Desire is the starting point of all achievement, not a hope, not a wish, but a keen pulsating desire which transcends everything.

Napoleon Hill

It is not in the still calm of life, or the repose of a pacific station, that great characters are formed. . . . The habits of a vigorous mind are formed in contending with difficulties. All history will convince you of this, and that wisdom and penetration are the fruit of experience, not the lessons of retirement and leisure. Great necessities call out great virtues.

John Adams

It is the Law that any difficulties that can come to you at any time, no matter what they are, must be exactly what you need most at the moment, to enable you to take the next step forward by overcoming them. The only real misfortune, the only real tragedy, comes when we suffer without learning the lesson.

Emmet Fox

Shared joy is a double joy; shared sorrow is half a sorrow.

Swedish proverb

Remember, we all stumble, every one of us. That's why it's a comfort to go hand in hand.

Emily Kimbrough

Oh, the comfort—the inexpressible comfort of feeling safe with a person—having neither to weigh thoughts nor measure words, but pouring them all right out, just as they are, chaff and grain together; certain that a faithful hand will take and sift them, keep what is worth keeping, and then with the breath of kindness blow the rest away.

Dinah Craik

I like her because she smiles at me and means it.

anonymous

Piglet sidled up to Pooh from behind. "Pooh!" he whispered. "Yes, Piglet?" "Nothing," said Piglet, taking Pooh's paw. "I just wanted to be sure of you.

A.A. Milne

No road is long with good company.

Turkish proverb

Soul-mates are people who bring out the best in you. They are not perfect but are always perfect for you.

anonymous

In the coldest February, as in every other month in every other year, the best thing to hold on to in this world is each other.

Linda Ellerbee

Treasure your relationships, not your possessions.

Anthony J. D'Angelo

Consider the following. We humans are social beings. We come into the world as the result of others' actions. We survive here in dependence on others. Whether we like it or not, there is hardly a moment of our lives when we do not benefit from others' activities. For this reason it is hardly surprising that most of our happiness arises in the context of our relationships with others.

Dalai Lama

The easiest period in a crisis situation is actually the battle itself. The most difficult is the period of indecision—whether to fight or run away. And the most dangerous period is the aftermath. It is then, with all his resources spent and his guard down that an individual must watch out for dulled reactions and faulty judgment.

Richard Nixon

I think my biggest achievement is that after going through a rather difficult time, I consider myself comparatively sane. I'm proud of that.

Jacqueline Kennedy Onassis

Meaning is not something you stumble across, like the answer to a riddle or the prize in a treasure hunt. Meaning is something you build into your life. You build it out of your own past, out of your affections and loyalties, out of the experience of humankind as it is passed on to you, out of your own talent and understanding, out of the things you believe in, out of the things and people you love, out of the values for which you are willing to sacrifice something. The ingredients are there. You are the only one who can put them together into that unique pattern that will be your life. Let it be a life that has dignity and meaning for you. If it does, then the particular balance of success or failure is of less account.

John W. Gardner

The Wise Woman's Stone

A wise woman who was traveling in the mountains found a precious stone in a stream. The next day she met another traveler who was hungry, and the wise woman opened her bag to share her food. The hungry traveler saw the precious stone and asked the woman to give it to him. She did so without hesitation. The traveler left, rejoicing in his good fortune. He knew the stone was worth enough to give him security for a lifetime. But a few days later he came back to return the stone to the wise woman. "I've been thinking," he said, "I know how valuable the stone is, but I give it back in the hope that you can give me something even more precious. Give me what you have within you that enabled you to give me the stone."

anonymous

Almost anybody can learn to think or believe or know, but not a single human being can be taught to be. Why? Because whenever you think or you believe or you know, you are a lot of other people: but the moment you are being, you're nobody-but-yourself. To be nobody-but-yourself, in a world which is doing its best night and day to make you everybody else, means to fight the hardest battle which any human being can fight, and never stop fighting . . . Does this sound dismal? It isn't. It's the most wonderful Life on earth.

e.e. cummings

Be patient toward all that is unsolved in your heart. Try to love the questions themselves. Do not now seek the answers which cannot be given because you would not be able to live them. And the point is to live everything. Live the questions now. Perhaps you will then gradually, without noticing it, live along some distant day into the answers.

Rainer Maria Rilke

Until one is committed, there is hesitancy, the chance to draw back, always ineffectiveness. Concerning all acts of initiative (and creation) there is one elementary truth the ignorance of which kills countless ideas and splendid plans: that the moment one definitely commits oneself, then providence moves too. All sorts of things occur to help one that would never otherwise have occurred. A whole stream of events issue from the decision raising in one's favour all manner of unforeseen incidents and meetings and material assistance, which no man could have dreamed would come his way. Whatever you can do or dream, you can begin it, boldness has genius, power and magic in it. Begin it now.

Johann Wolfgang von Goethe

My Acting Journal

My Acting Journal

My Acting Journal

My Acting Journal

My Acting Journal

My Acting Journal

My Acting Journal

About the Author

Larry Silverberg, director of the True Acting Institute, is one of the most widely published acting teachers in the world today and is considered one of the foremost authorities on the Sanford Meisner Technique of acting. He is the author of *The Sanford Meisner Approach: An Actors Workbook*, the internationally acclaimed four-volume series on the Meisner Technique. His other books include *Loving to Audition* and *The 7 Simple Truths of Acting for the Teen Actor*, all published by Smith and Kraus.

Silverberg is a graduate of the Neighborhood Playhouse where he studied with legendary acting teacher Sanford Meisner. Since then, Silverberg has worked professionally as an actor and director across the United States and in Canada. Most recently, Silverberg and his co-stars received high praise from the *New York Times* for their performances in Athol Fugard's *People Are Living There* at Signature Theatre Company in New York City, and Silverberg won the Seattle Critic's Association Stellar Acting Award for his portrayal of Teach in the Belltown Theatre Center production of David Mamet's *American Buffalo*.

Silverberg teaches acting in his world-renowned professional actors training program, The Meisner Intensive Training Program, which he holds at universities, colleges, and acting studios around the world. Silverberg is the founder of the True Acting Institute Association and is on the teaching faculties of The International Institute of the Performing Arts in Paris and European Act. Silverberg can be reached via his website: www.meisnerteacher.com

Other Books by Larry Silverberg

The Meisner Approach: An Actors Workbook

The Meisner Approach: Workbook Two
Emotional Freedom

The Meisner Approach: Workbook Three
Tackling the Text

The Meisner Approach: Workbook Four
Playing the Part

Loving to Audition

The 7 Simple Truths of Acting for the Teen Actor

Actors Resources from Larry Silverberg's True Acting Institute

Learn about Larry's acting programs for professional actors, acting teachers, and for college and high school acting students. On the Internet:

www.meisnerteacher.com

www.actorscraft.com

www.thewaybackout.com

And find the best college acting programs on Larry's website designed just for you:

www.collegeactingprograms.com

E-mail The True Acting Institute at
trueacting@actorscraft.com